	DATE DUE		

A Passion for Danger

A Passion for Danger

NANSEN'S ARCTIC ADVENTURES

Francine Jacobs

Illustrated with photographs, prints and maps

G. P. PUTNAM'S SONS NEW YORK

Illustration Credits

Farthest North, by Fridtjof Nansen, pp. 79, 94, 101, 104, 114, 124, 127, 131, 133, 142, 144.
The First Crossing of Greenland, by Fridtjof Nansen, pp. 35, 41, 42, 53, 56, 58.
Fridtiof Nansen, by N. C. Brøgger and Nordahl Rolfsen, pp. 18, 31, 69.
Hunting and Adventure in the Arctic, by Fridtjof Nansen, pp. 8, 15.
Norwegian Information Services, p. 84
The University of Oslo Library, pp. ix, 3, 6, 8, 23, 49, 61, 67, 81, 90, 99, 103, 110, 113, 116, 119, 130, 147, 149, 155.

G. P. Putnam's Sons, a division of The Putnam & Grosset Group,
200 Madison Avenue, New York, NY 10016.
G. P. Putnam's Sons, Reg. U.S. Pat. & Tm. Off.
Published simultaneously in Canada. Printed in the United States of America.
Book designed by Patrick Collins. Text set in Sabon.
Maps by Jeanyee Wong

Library of Congress Cataloging-in-Publication Data
Jacobs, Francine. A passion for danger : Nansen's Arctic adventures / Francine Jacobs.
p. cm. Includes bibliographical references.
Summary: A biography of the Norwegian explorer, author, scientist and statesman
who made many important expeditions to the North Pole.
1. Nansen, Fridtjof, 1861–1930—Juvenile literature. 2. Explorers—Norway—Biography—
Juvenile literature. 3. Arctic regions—Discovery and exploration—Juvenile literature. [1. Nansen, Fridtjof, 1861–1930. 2. Explorers. 3. Arctic regions—Discovery and exploration.] I. Title.
G635.N3J33 1994 93-5674 919.8—dc20 CIP [B] AC ISBN 0-399-22674-5

10 9 8 7 6 5 4 3 2 1

First Impression

To Julia Anne, with love

ACKNOWLEDGMENTS

The author wishes to thank the many individuals who assisted her research in Norway and made her visit there so productive. She is especially grateful to Kåre Berg, superintendent of the Fram Museum, Bygdøy, Oslo, for his tour of the ship and the Nansen collection and, most of all, for checking the manuscript of this book. Gratitude is also expressed to Elizabeth Fleischer Kåresen and Inger-Guri Fløgstad, librarians of the Nobel Institute, Oslo, for their help and to Grete Østgaard Lund, librarian, and Vladek Witek, photo conservator of the University of Oslo Library, for their assistance in obtaining photographs for this book.

Contents

Alone on the polar sea

The first great thing in life is to find yourself,
and for that you need solitude and contemplation,
at least sometimes.

—*Fridtjof Nansen*

CHAPTER ONE

Seed of the Viking

WHEN FRIDTJOF NANSEN was a boy growing up in Norway, he seemed to have everything he wanted. He loved to ski and skate and the long, northern winters brought plenty of snow and ice for that. He loved to hike and fish and the lingering sun of late spring and summer provided light long into the night for this. He was a happy boy, so much so that he came to believe he'd been born under a lucky star. Yet Fridtjof was never content for long. He had a restless spirit that set him apart and made him different from other children. It prodded him to try new things, to test himself. As he matured, this became a passion for danger that would lead him to great adventures.

Fridtjof was born on October 10, 1861, in a suburb of Christiania, the old name for the city that we know as Oslo. His parents chose his unusual name from an ancient Norse tale; Fridtjof of the saga was a daring Viking hero. To have a strange name that belonged to no one else you knew might have been a problem to some youngsters, but it never seemed to bother young Nansen. Besides, he quickly grew into a strong, self-assured lad no bully was likely to taunt.

Fridtjof lived in a large, comfortable farmhouse called Great Frøen that had been in his mother's family for some time. The household was busy with seven youngsters and a pet dog, Storm. Fridtjof had a younger brother, Alexander, and five older half brothers and sisters from his mother's previous marriage; her first husband had died. Outside, around the house, the yards and meadows were alive with farm animals: chickens, geese, pigs, horses, and cows. A river flowed near the front of the dwelling and, not far behind, a dense forest of pines, birches, and aspens stretched southward toward the city.

Fridtjof's father was a respected lawyer in their community of West Aker. Baldur Nansen was a short, slightly built, unathletic man who was cautious by nature. He took pride in being precise and thorough and, as one might guess, he was strict and old-fashioned as a parent.

Adelaide Nansen, Fridtjof's mother, was by contrast a sturdy, free-spirited person with a mind of her own. Born to privilege in an upper-class family, she had been left alone with five children to raise after the death of her first husband and had managed resourcefully on her own, before marrying Baldur Nansen. Adelaide was a capable homemaker. She sewed all her children's clothes herself, gardened in the spring and summer, and skied in winter despite social customs that frowned on grown-up women skiing; she could be seen wearing trousers beneath her long coat as she glided gracefully over the snow-covered countryside.

Fridtjof acquired valuable traits from each of his parents. His father taught him discipline and thoroughness. His mother inspired in him a spirit of adventure and a love of nature.

The natural world around him fascinated young Fridtjof. In summer, he often went down to the river that ran past his home and would wade in the cool, clear stream. He became a strong swimmer despite the coldness of the water. As if to

Fridtjof Nansen, nine years old

test his will, he would frequently plunge right in and try to coax his reluctant brother, Alexander, to join him.

In winter, the young brothers would play together on the river's frozen surface. More than once, Fridtjof, who was considerably bigger and stronger than Alexander, had to rescue his brother when he fell through the ice. In spring, the boys would dig for grubs and worms in their mother's garden. They would roll them up in the bottom of their breeches and return to the river with this bait to fish for minnows. At least twice, Fridtjof accidentally caught himself and came home with a fishhook stuck in his lower lip. Though it must have hurt, he never cried. Even when his mother used a razor to cut him free, he didn't flinch. Neither did he whimper when he cut his head and it bled heavily.

The more capable Fridtjof became, the more he sought challenge. With Alexander and Storm, he began to roam the surrounding countryside, hunting squirrels with a toy bow and arrow. Fridtjof had a natural skill for skiing. He had learned to ski on a pair of sawed-off, hand-me-down skis when he was only four. He used these until a good-hearted neighbor made him some sturdy, ash-wood skis of his own to replace them and gave him a pole; skiers used only one pole then. By the time he was seven, Fridtjof regularly skied to school in Christiania and home again, a distance of five miles round-trip each day.

Near his home was a place called Huseby Hill where meets were held. Fridtjof and his brothers were forbidden to ski there because it was a steep slope with a dangerous jump; only the best skiers dared to try Huseby. Fridtjof admired the experts who sped down the hill, soared high into the air, and landed on their skis near the bottom. He wanted to be like them.

One day, Fridtjof made his way over to Huseby and climbed halfway up the hill. From there, he managed to ski down safely—but still, he wasn't satisfied. So, despite his parents' warning and the danger, he climbed all the way to the top next time and, as onlookers gasped, he pushed off. Down he sped, zooming toward the jump. Then, all at once, he was flying through the air. The flight ended with a fall in a deep bank of snow. There he lay buried waist deep and motionless. The spectators thought he had surely broken his neck. But Fridtjof rose, shook off the snow, and retrieved his skis which had come free. Boys over the whole hillside broke into laughter directed at him, and Fridtjof was embarrassed.

He was not one to be easily discouraged, however. Fridtjof returned to Huseby to try the hill again. He practiced until, at last, he mastered the jump and was even allowed to participate in the meets. In fact, one day, he won a prize. But that day the famed Telemark county skiers who used no pole at all had also competed. Their feats were so outstanding that Fridtjof made little of his own triumph and didn't even take his prize home. He was forming high personal standards for success, it seemed, and a hero had to be the very best at what he did.

Whatever Fridtjof undertook, he usually finished, but no sooner was he done with one thing, than he was on to another. He was venturesome like his mother but also practical like his father. Once, for example, young Fridtjof and Alexander were permitted to go alone to the annual fair in Christiania. The boys were excited and looked forward to the grand event. Their parents, grandmother, and aunt gave them some money to treat themselves to a good time. The fair was filled with various kinds of entertainment. There were booths with clowns, magicians, and jugglers, and counters where the children could purchase toys, candies, and tempting gingerbread cakes. The two brothers viewed it all with wonder but kept their money deep in their pockets. They were saving it to buy something special. On their way home, they stopped at a market and purchased what they wanted most of all, some tools.

At home, their family was surprised by the boys' restraint. Such self-discipline deserved a reward. So Fridtjof and Alexander were sent back with more money to spend to enjoy themselves. And what did they do? They bought more tools.

Not all Fridtjof's behavior, however, was praiseworthy. He would dawdle and become so absorbed in his thoughts that he could take forever to get dressed in the morning. And at dinner he was sometimes so preoccupied that he lost track of the conversation around the table. He could be so distracted that he might eat anything, even a rotten egg that had been accidentally served to him.

His curiosity could be irritating, too. Fridtjof might ask, "Why?" "But why?" so many times before he was satisfied that he would become a nuisance. And his constant tinkering

Great Frøen, with nine-year-old Fridtjof standing to the left of his parents in the garden of his childhood home, 1870

could be maddening, too. One day, an expensive new sewing machine arrived at the house. But it was hardly there before Fridtjof had taken it apart. When his mother came home that day, it was completely disassembled and lay in pieces on the floor.

The Nansens were not poor, but they lived modestly as a matter of principle. Baldur Nansen expected the children to do their share of the household chores. All of them took turns serving at the table at mealtimes. Each received a small allowance and was expected to spend it wisely. Fridtjof learned to value the things he had and to make them last. He didn't grow up accustomed to luxuries and cared little for them or, for that matter, for food or much else beyond his basic needs. He never put great value on anything he could do without.

What really excited Fridtjof was adventure. From the time he was ten, he would go on weekend camping trips with his older brothers. On Saturday afternoons in May, after their dinner, the boys would gather bread, butter, bits of sausage, and coffee, and start on their way at about three o'clock. They would walk for about five hours over tough, hilly land through the woods toward certain trout streams. The journey was especially rigorous because they hiked quickly to cover the distance while it was light. When they finally reached their destination, the tired lads were always much more eager to fish than to rest. They would wade right into the water and fish into the dim, early hours of morning. When the boys finally had to sleep, they would lie down in a hunter's hut or under a sheltering tree. In a few hours, they would be back fishing in the river again.

Fridtjof loved these times in the wilderness. He would hop from stone to stone in the river or wade waist deep in the chilling stream. There was fun, horseplay, and camaraderie. The boys joked and told stories around the campfire as their catch broiled over the embers. Fridtjof pitched in and shared eagerly in whatever had to be done.

As he matured, Fridtjof began to go off into the woods on his own, alone. His hikes would take him farther and farther and last longer. One fall, he took Alexander with him to hunt hare. The two young brothers stalked their prey on the frost-hardened ground and hardly slept. They were gone thirteen days, for the last few of which they had little but meager rations of potato cakes to eat. When they finally returned home, they were bone tired and starved.

Fridtjof continued to trek into the wilderness on foot and on skis. He seemed determined to test his endurance. As a young teenager he would spend weeks camping in the forest alone, taking with him few supplies, preferring instead to forage for his food. He learned to improvise and to make do with what he found. He never seemed discontented or lonely

Nansen at seventeen

in the woods; the peace and solitude pleased him. Learning how to survive in the natural world appealed to something deep within him. He was always ready to go off and ski twenty miles or more without any food or thought of hunger.

In school, however, Fridtjof's grades were only average. The forest was the classroom he preferred. Hunting grouse, ptarmigan, and hare, fishing, and learning to live off the land were the lessons about which he cared most. The outdoors life seemed to call him and lead him toward a career in natural science.

In 1880, at age eighteen, Fridtjof entered the university in Christiania. He was by now a tall, modest, confident young man. His teenage adventures in the wilderness had come to an end, but they were not forgotten; for, deep down, the seed of Viking ancestors had taken root.

CHAPTER TWO

A Season in the Arctic

THERE WERE A GREAT many subjects to choose from at the university, so Nansen found himself pulled in different directions because of his extraordinary curiosity. When at last he had to select his course of study, his interest in nature finally won him over; he would prepare for a career in zoology, the study of animal life. This might provide him with the opportunity to do fieldwork in the outdoors he loved so much.

In January 1882, Nansen went to discuss his plans with his adviser, Professor Robert Collett. The older zoologist listened to his ambitions and advised the eager twenty-year-old to join a sealing expedition for a season in the Arctic as he himself had done as a student. Nansen saw the advantages of acquiring field experience, but it was undoubtedly the promise of adventure that was persuasive.

Two months later, when his academic courses were completed, Nansen boarded the *Viking*, a large, new sealer, at a port south of Christiania. What an odd sight he must have been to Captain Krefting and his crew, this tall, clean-cut, blond youth carrying nets, dipping and dredging devices, a telescope, microscope, camera, sketch pad, and various instruments and containers for collecting and examining specimens. But the tough, weathered sealers who well knew the dangers ahead in the stormy Arctic seas reserved their judgment of the young stranger. Nansen would have to prove his worth to win their respect.

The *Viking* was a ship designed for one purpose only: to penetrate the icy waters of the north. Sturdy and powerful, it was driven by sails and a coal-burning steam engine. The sealer carried a crew of sixty-two men, including the captain and Nansen, who would spend the next five months living and working together. At sunrise, on March 11, 1882, the *Viking* edged out from its wharf and slowly cleared port as its single stack spewed out plumes of sooty, black smoke.

Nansen stood on deck watching as the ship turned out to sea. It was quite a change for a country boy who had freely roamed the silent, pine-scented forests to be standing there on the rolling, creaking deck of a sealer facing into the salty, spray-laden wind.

The sealer Viking *seeking passage through the ice*

The *Viking* was a hunter. The men who ventured out to sea on her relied on finding seals for their livelihood. The seals were valued for their pelts, leathery hides, and oil. At first the men would seek the newborn pups of the saddleback seal. It was necessary to locate the main breeding grounds of the saddleback in time to catch the pups, or "white coats," on the drift ice before they shed their long wool and took to the water. The soft, white coats of the newborns fetched high prices. So the *Viking* laid on full sail and the stokers fed the boilers furiously. The ship traveled northward from the North Sea into the Norwegian Sea. The site of the main breeding grounds, or Great Bight as it was known, shifted about with the drift ice in the region of Norway's Jan Mayen island. Each year it had to be found anew.

For seven days, the *Viking* plowed on through calm and clear weather and through dense fogs and storms in hopes of finding the Great Bight by the end of March when the pups were born. Try as he might to adjust to the lurching rhythms of the ship, Nansen experienced seasickness and was miserable. Finally, from the white, barrel-shaped crow's nest high atop the mainmast, he heard the lookout call, "Ice ahead!"

Though it was night, Nansen peered out into the blackness. As his eyes adjusted to the dark, he made out the first slabs of ice floating on the sea. Soon there were more of them; clusters of white ice floes surrounded the ship. Then came a strange, roaring sound in the distance, like the noise of a great waterfall approaching. Nansen learned that the din came from ice floes, crashing and colliding as powerful currents carried them southward toward the *Viking*.

As he listened to the awesome sound, Nansen observed an unusual lightening in the northern sky produced by the reflection of the ice fields below onto clouds above. His shipmates called this "ice blink." It signals that the sea ahead is packed with ice, he learned. The Arctic skies, he was also told, offer other valuable clues to conditions beneath them. Where the sky is dark blue, it is likely that the sea below is open and ice free; this is called "water sky."

The ice made Nansen more wary of his new environment. But he became conscious also of the Arctic's immense beauty: the red glow of the sun shining on the sea, the pure white gleaming ice, and the ever-changing patterns of light in the sky above. The birds attracted him; different kinds of gulls swooped and darted around the sealer, their slender legs and webbed feet gracefully folded under them. There were songbirds, too—small, white snow buntings noisily hopping about and pecking in the snow on the ice floes.

Locating the Great Bight proved to be difficult. Captain Krefting spent hours high in the crow's nest peering through a long telescope, searching in vain for the breeding grounds. Meanwhile Nansen lowered dip nets into open stretches of water to sample animal life in the frigid sea. He netted and dredged up varieties of small marine animals to examine under his microscope and to describe. He also captured birds to study and took the temperature of the water at different depths. The wonder of the Arctic, the splendor of the open ice fields, the vast emptiness and solitude strangely reminded Nansen of the contentment he had known in the forest wilderness near home.

In addition to his scientific research, Nansen participated in some of the crew's work. On April 1, for example, he helped to "roll" the ship. Rolling was a technique used to free a sealer when it became stuck in the ice. The crew of the vessel, often aided by sailors from other sealers in the area, would gather on one side of the jammed ship. Then, on a signal from the captain, they would rush to the other side and back again and again, rocking the vessel until the ice released it.

Other sealers were also searching for the Great Bight. One evening in the moonlight, a crewman pointed out a particular vessel to Nansen. It was the *Vega,* a ship of some renown.

Four years earlier, Adolf Erik Nordenskiøld, a famous Swedish explorer and geologist, had sailed the *Vega* eastward and navigated the treacherous, ice-choked waters above the northern coast of Siberia. In 1879, Nordenskiøld passed through the Bering Strait to Japan. This historic voyage had opened a "Northeast Passage" to the Orient.

The *Viking* searched but could not locate the Great Bight. By the end of April, the effort had become pointless. The crew watched in envy as other sealers, laden with sealskins, passed by. "Where on earth have you been?" their skippers called to Captain Krefting. One ship boasted of some twelve thousand pelts; another, fourteen thousand. As it turned out, because of the fog, the *Viking* had missed the prime sealing ground by a mere four miles.

The search turned now to hunting small groups of seals on ice floes. This was not very productive, so the *Viking* came about and proceeded in a southwesterly direction toward Iceland, approaching close enough for Nansen to see its glistening glaciers and the dark, volcanic peaks of its offshore islands. The *Viking* sailed into Denmark Strait, the stretch of sea between Iceland and Greenland. There on the drifting ice, bladdernose seals were found. These were actually hooded seals, but the sealers called them bladdernoses because of a sac of skin attached to the male's nose that looked like a bright red balloon, or bladder, when inflated.

The *Viking* lowered its boats with hunters. The men were dressed in warm, woolen clothes, canvas overalls, and high sea boots. Each boat's crew consisted of five or six sailors. One, the coxswain, stood at the rear of the boat steering the craft with a long oar. Three or four men rowed. The rowers carried skinning knives and sharpening steels slung from their waists; they would skin the seals. They also had spiked seal clubs. At the front of the boat stood the gunner with his rifle at the ready; he directed the crew. Nansen became a gunner on one of the *Viking*'s ten boats.

Searching for seals

Hunting the bladdernose was a strange ritual. The large, docile seal was generally found lying alone on the ice, but its range extended greatly, covering enormous areas. At the hunters' approach, the creature would stir, wriggle over to the edge of the ice, and prepare to dive into the sea. At this point, the rowers would utter a loud, unearthly call, causing the animal to pause uncertainly. If the bladdernose got set to plunge again, the rowers tried to stop the animal with a second chorus in another key. By then it was hoped that the gunner had closed in within range to shoot the seal on the ice where the skinners could get to it. If a seal were shot in the water, the skinners would rapidly haul the animal with their seal clubs to the ice before it sank.

When the hunt went well, the ice was bloody and littered with seal carcasses and the men quickly stripped the bodies of their valuable skins and blubber. The savagery of the hunt disgusted Nansen, but he did not shrink from it. Once the butchery was done, the boats departed for the *Viking*, leaving behind the remains for the gulls to feast upon. The daily hunts went on for weeks from the end of May well into June, and thousands of seal skins were taken.

The success of the hunt in Denmark Strait did much to make up for the crew's disappointment at missing the Great Bight earlier. Their spirits lightened and they joked, played games, and swapped stories when they weren't working. Nansen's contribution to the hunt, particularly his excellent marksmanship, made him popular. Though he was of a very different social class from his rough, uneducated shipmates, Nansen was at ease among them. He and the captain sometimes joined the crew in games, and the two spent even more time together talking. Nansen was eager to learn more about the Arctic, and Captain Krefting enjoyed sharing his experiences with the young scientist; the men became good friends.

Toward the end of June before the seal hunting was done, misfortune struck the *Viking* again. The ship became jammed in ice moving down the east coast of Greenland. The *Viking* and its crew were trapped, imprisoned in the ice pack, unable to continue sealing. There was danger, too.

The pressures of the ice posed a constant threat to the hull of the ship. Many sailors worried that even if the vessel held together they would eventually run out of provisions and starve. Captain Krefting tried to keep up the crew's morale, but, as the days dragged on into weeks, the men's concerns increased.

Nansen, however, refused to despair. He encouraged his shipmates with a hopeful attitude and continued his research, sampling the waters beneath the ice and dredging for bottom creatures. When he wasn't working, he joined others in venturing out onto the ice pack to hunt bears. Bear meat, he believed, might be an answer to the problem of their dwindling supplies.

Arctic bears are known as ice bears or polar bears. These huge, creamy white carnivores feed mainly on seals and possess great strength and agility. They are also adept swimmers, capable of diving to the sea floor to bring up kelp and mussels. On the Arctic drift ice, camouflaged in their natural snowsuits, they wander great distances to hunt. Nansen used his keen eyesight and his daring and marksmanship to kill fourteen bears. The hunt added to his reputation and to the ship's provisions; though many men refused to eat bear meat in the mistaken belief that it was poisonous, others gladly feasted on bear steaks, tongues, and hearts.

While the *Viking* was icebound, Nansen became fascinated with the beauty of Greenland nearby. He gazed at it from the crow's nest on high. This vast land was only twenty-five to thirty miles to the west of the ship, and its rugged features, the jagged mountain spires, or *nunataks,* that seemed to burst upward through the inland ice cap, were clearly visible to him. Through his telescope he studied the bare peaks and the glaciers that pushed between the mountains down to the sea, and made drawings of what he saw. He also wrote of the land's "wild beauty" in his diary. The attractions of this unexplored, forbidding place so captivated him that he wanted to hike across the treacherous drift ice all the way to the coast.

Captain Krefting, however, would not permit it. He could not let Nansen leave the vessel for the length of time such a trek might require. But Nansen yearned to set foot on the icy coast that seemed to draw him. He thought it possible to

Drift ice

reach the shore if he were able to drag a light boat over the ice. One day he would return, perhaps, to try it and then go on to penetrate the barrier mountains before him and explore Greenland's mysterious interior.

In mid-July, after drifting for twenty-four days, the pack ice finally broke up, freeing the *Viking*. The sealing season was over by now, and so the ship headed home to port. For many years afterward, whenever there was talk of this dangerous voyage, the sealers would refer to it as the "Nansen trip" and recount stories of the adventure they had shared with him.

CHAPTER THREE

Greenland Beckons

WHEN NANSEN RETURNED HOME from his sealing voyage, his adviser, Professor Collett, recommended him for the position of curator of the zoological collection at the museum in the city of Bergen, on Norway's west coast. It was a big boost to Nansen's career because he was only twenty years old and had yet to publish a single scientific paper. When the job was offered to him, he accepted it and determined he would make good and be worthy of Collett's faith in him.

Nansen found it difficult, however, to adjust to the inactive, indoor life of a curator; nonetheless, he persevered. Day after day he labored at his microscope, studying tiny insects, taking care to describe and classify them accurately. The task took endless hours of concentration, and he was forced to withdraw from virtually all his other interests.

In October 1882, after a few months at the museum, Nansen wrote to his father that he had begun to feel like a "first-class stick-in-the-mud." Despite his commitment, however, it was not possible for him to shackle his mind completely.

So it was that one evening eleven months later, in September 1883, Nansen read with unusual interest a newspaper account of the safe return of Baron Nordenskiøld from an expedition to Greenland. This was the Swedish explorer's second attempt to investigate the interior of this land where he had hoped to find an ice-free, green oasis.

According to the report, Nordenskiøld and his party had trekked inland from a base camp near the settlement of Christianshaab on the west coast and had traveled a distance of some eighty miles, finding nothing but snow and ice. They had set up a field camp where Nordenskiøld waited while scouts were sent out on skis to explore the area farther to the east. He had instructed them to locate the greenbelt and to bring back samples of the plant life. The scouts were two Laplanders. Lapps (or Samis, as they are known today) are people native to the Arctic regions of Norway, Sweden, Finland, and nearby Russia. The Lapps Nordenskiøld had sent were swift and tireless skiers. By their own account, they had traveled about one hundred fifty miles without finding any sign of an oasis; they had returned empty-handed.

The story intrigued Nansen. He recalled the stark beauty of that frozen land he had observed from the sealer. But he was somewhat skeptical about the distance the scouts claimed to have explored. He began to think about crossing Greenland on skis himself, and the idea excited him.

For the time being, however, it was back to work at the museum. Nansen continued his research and, as time passed, became increasingly competent in his scientific skills. He worked hard until Christmas before taking some time for recreation. Over the holidays, he visited a friend in Bergen with whom he enjoyed talking, listening to music, and reading poetry. In a happy mood, he was likely to recite passages from his favorite work, *Fridtiof's Saga,* the adventures of his namesake.

Nansen had matured by now into a tall, blond man with rugged, handsome features, piercing gray-blue eyes, and a light mustache that swept downward at its ends. He liked to walk quickly and was conscious of his impressive appearance; it pleased him. He usually wore a sporting cap and an unconventional, close-fitting tunic, a wool jacket with a high collar and a row of buttons that ran from his right shoulder to below his waist. He never wore an overcoat no matter how cold the weather. His appearance was an embarrassment to his brother, Alexander, who dressed like other men of the time in a more formal suit coat and vest, striped trousers, and a high silk hat.

Though he enjoyed brief holidays and took time to sketch at the studio of a friend, Nansen's work continued to be confining. He missed the outdoor life and found little opportunity for it in Bergen. The coastal city's mild, rainy climate made the area unsuitable for his favorite pastime, skiing. He keenly felt a need to do something physical and out-of-doors. Then one evening, late in January 1884, he read about a ski meet to be held in a matter of days at Huseby Hill back home. All of a sudden, he knew he must compete in the contest. So he hastily arranged time off from the museum and made plans to go.

There was still no road or rail link through the mountains between Bergen and Christiania at that time. So Nansen could travel only by train to the nearby town of Voss. From there, eastward to the capital, overland passage was all but impossible. No matter; having made up his mind to go, Nansen decided to make the trip on his own, on skis. He ignored the pleas of friends who tried to talk him out of it. Such a trip across some one hundred fifty miles of steep, treacherous mountains would be madness, they argued. But Nansen took the train to Voss and with his dog, Flink, and a few provisions, struck out on skis for Christiania.

His journey defies description, for the area through which he had to pass is a maze of rock-strewn, misty mountains and steep, natural passages gouged by centuries of glacial action.

Even in summertime, much of the region is bare of vegetation and inhospitable. In winter, there is the risk of falling off icy ridges and the constant danger of rock slides and avalanches. Nevertheless, with extraordinary skill, instinct, and raw nerve, Nansen pressed on. It took six days of heroic effort, but he made it through and arrived in time to enter the Huseby competition; he was rewarded by winning a prize. When the meet was over, he retraced his hazardous trip on skis back to Voss.

The incredible journey of negotiating the narrow mountain passes, facing death at every turn, was more than a foolhardy escapade. The feat meant something deeper, more spiritual, to Nansen. He described his feelings in a letter to his father. "One feels here that one stands alone, face-to-face with Nature and God."

Back in Bergen, Nansen resumed his less-adventurous life at the museum. He lived at the home of a childless couple named Holdt. Reverend Holdt and his wife were extremely fond of him and treated him like a son. They nicknamed him Esau, for Esau in the bible was known to be a hunter and outdoorsman.

Nansen learned another kind of courage from the Holdts. Reverend Holdt provided spiritual comfort to victims of the dread sickness, leprosy, or Hansen's disease. This fatal illness is caused by a germ that attacks the skin, nerves, and other tissues, leading to deformities and disfigurement. Although people feared the disease and shunned lepers, Reverend Holdt attended to them with love and charity. His inspiring example made an impression on Nansen that would, one day, influence his own life's work.

Meanwhile, one evening in November 1884, Nansen read a newspaper article reporting the finding of bits of wreckage from an American ship, *Jeannette,* that had been lost on an expedition in the Arctic Ocean. The *Jeannette* had been searching for a passage through the ice to the North Pole

Nansen in his tunic at twenty-seven

when, in 1881, it had become trapped in the pack ice, crushed, and destroyed north of Siberia.

Nansen was curious about the location of the debris, for the wreckage had come ashore on the southwest coast of Greenland almost three thousand miles from the site of the sinking. How did it get there? he wondered.

Professor Henrik Mohn, an expert on weather and the atmosphere and a respected meteorologist, suggested that an ocean current had carried the debris. He conjectured that the current must have coursed westward through the Arctic Ocean and then veered south to sweep around the southern tip of Greenland. This was a bold proposal because little was known about the polar region and its currents then. It was bound to stir up controversy.

Nansen was attracted to Mohn's theory. If Mohn were right, then it might be possible to use this current to explore the area of the Pole, he thought. The idea aroused his imagination, but, for the time being, Nansen's attention remained focused on his studies. He continued his research, describing marine creatures such as worms, crustaceans, mollusks, and certain fish, and prepared for his doctoral degree in zoology.

Nansen had begun to publish his work in scientific journals, and his papers were well received. Opportunities to do research elsewhere, including in the United States, came his way, but he chose to remain where he was for the time being. His mother had died some years earlier, and his elderly father was not well. Baldur Nansen, in fact, died in April of 1885, freeing Fridtjof to travel. So the following spring, in 1886, he took three months off from the museum to go to Naples in southern Italy. He paid for this trip in a novel way. The year before, he had won a gold medal for a scientific investigation of certain sea worms. But before accepting it, he asked to have the award cast in less precious copper and to be given the difference in cash. This he put toward the expenses of his trip.

In Naples, Nansen joined other scientists at work at a new marine research center. This was the first of its kind to keep living sea creatures in large aquaria for the public to view and for scientific study. Nansen remained in Italy for three months. When he wasn't working, he spent his leisure hours relaxing with his colleagues, chatting and dancing in cafes. He loved to dance and his laughter was a familiar sound amid the din and gaiety on balmy, spring evenings.

Nansen had been so impressed with the scientific value of the center in Naples that, when he returned to Bergen, he urged authorities to build similar facilities in Norway. He resumed his work at the museum. Almost immediately, however, his attention was diverted once again to Greenland. He had become fascinated by yet another attempt to probe the unexplored interior of that island. An expedition led by an American, Robert E. Peary, and a Dane, Christian Maigaard, had ventured eastward, inland, on a route similar to Nordenskiøld's. Peary sought to learn more about the Greenland ice cap and whether it might extend northward to provide access to the Pole.

As it turned out, Peary's expedition penetrated about one hundred and ten miles into the interior, which rose steadily to form a central plateau; his party climbed to an elevation of 7,525 feet, almost a mile and a half high. Altogether they had spent twenty-three days on the ice before returning to their home base in the west.

It was prudent for explorers to begin crossing Greenland from the west coast. Eskimos, as Inuit people of that area were then called, and Danish colonists had settlements there and could provide care and shelter. The east coast was desolate and much less accessible. Ships could not approach the land there because of the heavy ice offshore. Even if a party could be put ashore, it could not depend on receiving help.

Nansen took particular notice that Peary and Maigaard, and Nordenskiøld earlier, had all reported that beyond the fringe of rifted ice there appeared to be a smooth, flat expanse of snow reaching out toward the yet-unseen center of Greenland. It could be crossed on skis, he thought, recalling his past ambition. Once more, Greenland, the mysterious land he had glimpsed from the *Viking*, seemed to beckon him.

If he were to explore the island, Nansen decided, he would not start from the west coast as others had; they had burdened themselves with supplies for a round trip, out and back. No, he would land on the east coast and proceed westward. His party, therefore, would merely need provisions for one way and should be able to travel lighter and faster. The idea, however, involved far greater risk, for such an expedition could only go forward; there could be no retreat, no rescue. Failure would mean certain death.

But the dangers of such an undertaking did not dissuade Nansen. The more he considered the matter, in fact, the more the challenge appealed to him. He shared his thoughts with friends, who tried to discourage him, but he argued with them and became stubbornly convinced that he could do it. Bit by bit, his ideas developed into a plan. On an impulse, he traveled to Stockholm to discuss it with Nordenskiøld.

The Swedish capital was cold and snowy that November 3, 1887, when Nansen, without so much as an overcoat, arrived in his odd, tight-fitting tunic. He appeared at the prestigious Academy of Science without an appointment and asked to see Nordenskiøld. Nansen was shown to a laboratory where "old man Nor," as he was affectionately known, was studying minerals. The celebrated geologist paused to take in the oddly dressed Norwegian who had come to meet him. The two spoke briefly and agreed to talk again later in the evening.

Nordenskiøld listened to the young scientist and questioned him carefully. He was skeptical at first about Nansen's unorthodox plan but was impressed with him nonetheless. Nansen was plainspoken, direct, and clearly no uninformed adventurer; he was also physically fit and keen to undertake the expedition. The more they spoke, the more Nordenskiøld's doubts subsided. Finally the elderly explorer was persuaded that Nansen could succeed, and he decided to help him.

Nordenskiøld shared his hard-earned knowledge of Greenland, and the two talked late into the night. He was pleased that someone, at last, might find the green oasis that he still believed to be at the center of that frozen land. He encouraged Nansen and wished him well. Before they parted, the older man made a warm, friendly gesture; he promised to send Nansen a pair of Arctic boots for the journey.

CHAPTER FOUR

A Madman's Scheme

ENCOURAGED BY NORDENSKIØLD'S SUPPORT, Nansen returned to Bergen determined to make the Greenland expedition. But first he would need financial backing for the project. He decided to write to the University Council in Christiania and put his proposal before them. On November 11, 1887, he began: "It is my intention next summer to undertake a journey across the inland ice of Greenland from the east to the west coast," and then he went on to describe what he would need for the expedition. Mindful of the frugal nature of his countrymen, he asked for the relatively modest sum of 5,000 crowns for expenses (about 30,500 U.S. dollars today).

The council reacted to Nansen's request with interest and recommended that their colleague's bold proposal be approved. But members of the parliament had other concerns. Many feared that voters in their home districts might view the expedition as a foolhardy adventure and a wasteful extravagance. The plan had a good chance of failure, as they saw it, and they were not about to share the risk by putting their own political careers in danger. A government publication came out against the proposal; it questioned why the Norwegian people should spend their money "in order that a private individual might treat himself to a pleasure trip to Greenland." The doubters prevailed. Nansen's request was refused.

Indeed, those who opposed it went even further, attacking the plan as a madman's scheme and ridiculing Nansen. Articles critical of him appeared in the press. A popular paper in Bergen carried this comic advertisement:

> Notice.—In the month of June next, Curator Nansen will give a snow-shoe [skiing] display, with long jumps on the Inland Ice of Greenland. Reserved seats in the crevasses [deep cracks]. Return ticket unnecessary.

Nansen was surprised by the harshness of the attacks upon him. "Most people . . . considered it simple madness . . . and were convinced that I was either not quite right in the head or was simply tired of life." Despite public opinion and a chorus of criticism, he never wavered in his determination to undertake the journey.

Nor was the fuss about his proposal confined to Norway. In England, the London press mocked him, too. And in Copenhagen, a Danish explorer lectured, ". . . it is ten to one that either Nansen will throw away his own life, and perhaps the lives of others, to no purpose."

Nansen's plan was indeed full of risk; there was no denying that it had a potential for disaster, and people knew it. What no one could know was the strength of Nansen's will. Despite the scorn that was heaped upon him, or perhaps even because of it, he held fast to his plan.

Only one piece in a Danish newspaper supported him. It was written by a Norwegian geologist named Armand Helland who had visited Greenland himself. Helland wrote that

Nansen's expedition could succeed. It would require an especially capable leader, excellent skiers, and equipment designed to meet the severe conditions of the inland ice cap. Although the journey would be hazardous, all the twenty or so explorers who had already ventured into the interior had managed to return safely, he reminded readers.

It happened that a wealthy Danish merchant, Augustin Gamél, read Helland's piece and was persuaded by it. On January 12, 1888, he sent word to the University Council in Christiania that he would personally back the expedition. He offered to grant the funds Nansen needed.

Nansen was thrilled to have Gamél's financial support and quickly accepted the offer. With this encouragement, he tried next to win over the doubting public. He offered information and described his plan more fully to the press. He wanted people to know that though the perils of the expedition were great, he was confident that he could overcome them and that he fully intended to survive and to succeed. In all likelihood, however, his stubborn pride played a part in his determination to accept the challenge; he was undoubtedly prepared to gamble with his life and those of his party to prove he was right.

Now assured of financial backing, Nansen developed his plans. He began to think about sleds, equipment, and supplies that the expedition would require. He would select three or four men, all excellent skiers, to form his team. In the first months of 1888, even as some publications continued to criticize the venture as a harebrained scheme, Nansen advertised to recruit his party. Forty men responded from whom Nansen chose three sturdy Norwegians. The first, Otto Sverdrup, was thirty-two; he was a tall, round-shouldered, red-bearded fellow who was an experienced sea captain. Sverdrup seemed mature, stable, and likely to be a reliable companion. He brought another able recruit to Nansen, a younger man, twenty-three, named Christian Christiansen

Trana. Trana worked on the Sverdrups' family farm in central Norway. On the strength of Sverdrup's enthusiastic recommendation, Nansen accepted Trana.

The third chosen was a thirty-one-year-old army officer, Oluf Dietrichson. Competent and self-disciplined, Dietrichson seemed likely to perform well amid whatever hardships lay ahead. To round out the team, Nansen decided to follow Nordenskiøld's example and take two Laplanders. So he wrote to men in the northern Norwegian province of Finmarken and asked them to find two hardy Mountain Lapps for him. Nansen wanted the dangers of the venture to be explained in advance to them and requested that the Lapps be unmarried, mature, and thirty to forty years old.

The members of the expedition

Meanwhile, the bleak, chilly weeks of that winter in Bergen were busy. In addition to working on details for the expedition, Nansen was also preparing to qualify for his doctoral degree in zoology. In the spring, he would formally defend his academic thesis before a faculty committee in Christiania. He split his time between his research on the nervous system of animals, on the one hand, and planning for the Greenland expedition, on the other. Both concerns were vital to him, but it was difficult not to spend more time on the expedition. "I would rather take a bad degree than have a bad outfit," he confided to a friend.

In planning the trek across the inland ice, Nansen tried to imagine every contingency. Any matter unforeseen, any detail omitted might have disastrous consequences. He designed and supervised the construction of an amphibious craft, a light boat with steel runners attached to the hull that could carry the group, its gear, and supplies through the coastal waters and be pulled like a sled over the ice. He rejected the idea of taking reindeer or dogs along to do the hauling. There wasn't time to obtain good huskies and it would be difficult, in any event, to get animals ashore; they would also require additional provisions. He decided that the men themselves would have to tow the sleds. This limited greatly what could be taken. Only essential supplies and light, durable gear could accompany them.

Nansen's knack for mechanical things and his considerable experience in the rugged countryside of his youth served him well in assembling his equipment. From accounts of earlier Arctic expeditions, he learned that their sleds had been heavy and clumsy. The runners of the sleds had been narrow and had sunk into soft snow, making them difficult to pull. So Nansen set out to design a better sled. He built a light, sturdy one with wide, skilike wooden runners shod with steel plates. In all, he made five sleds that were almost identical. Each was crafted from hard ash wood and assembled without nails, with leather lashings used instead to make them flexible. At the rear end, he gave each a wide, arching handle to make it easy to steer and push. The sleds were about nine and a half feet long by one and a half feet wide, and they weighed only about twenty-eight pounds.

Nansen tested out his equipment in the frigid mountains and on the high plateau behind Bergen. In addition to the sleds, he tried out a three-man sleeping bag of reindeer skin he had designed, a five-piece tent he had obtained from Copenhagen, and a brass cooker. This small, alcohol camp stove, which he also had designed, contained chambers to warm food and to melt snow for drinking water at the same time. To provide additional water, he perfected a curved, metal flask to be fit against each man's body. The vessel would be filled with snow at the start of each march so that the heat of the day's exertions would produce water.

He outfitted the expedition with specially made light boots and chose strong hardwood skis and two kinds of snowshoes, the familiar paddle type and Norwegian *truger* that are made of willow twigs braided in a small hardwood frame. He selected complete sets of clothes from woolen underwear to waterproof outerwear. He picked eye shields with narrow slits, smoked-glass goggles, and red silk veils to protect everyone from the glare of the sun and its reflection from the ice and snow.

Nansen assembled his provisions with care. He chose foods such as liver pâté, biscuits of meat powder and of oatmeal, cakes of meat chocolate (four-fifths chocolate, one-fifth dried meat), jam, condensed soup and milk, coffee, sugar, and—most important of all—pemmican. Pemmican, the staple of all Arctic sled expeditions, is made of dried meat and fat shaped into blocks. To get the best pemmican, Nansen traveled to Copenhagen. Ironically, however, his order was filled incorrectly and he wasn't to learn until too late that the fat, so necessary to supply calories of body heat in the cold, had been omitted.

The remainder of his kit consisted of scientific instruments, guns, ammunition, a camera, watches, tools, tarpaulins, bamboo poles, rope, and such items as candles, matches, diaries, sewing needles, and a sail maker's palm: a type of thimble used in sewing canvas. Altogether the expedition's kit weighed about 1,200 pounds. It had taken months to outfit the expedition and to prepare for the journey.

Nansen traveled to Christiania to present the first of his lectures in the final process toward his doctoral degree. Meanwhile, only two weeks remained before the day the explorers were to depart. But the Lapps who were to join them had yet to appear. Finally, when they did arrive, via boat to the port city of Trondheim and then by train to Christiania, they were not at all what Nansen had expected.

One Lapp, Ole Ravna, was a short man in his mid-forties, married, with five children. The other was a river fisherman of twenty-seven named Samuel Balto. Neither spoke Norwegian well, and both men had come merely to earn the money. To Nansen's dismay, the Lapps had only just learned from other passengers on the train about their destination. Now that they knew the dangers ahead, they were terrified. Each was convinced that he'd never see his home again. Because there wasn't time to replace them, however, Nansen worked to overcome their fears and convince them to come along. Warily, Ravna and Balto agreed to join the party.

Nansen completed the defense of his thesis within days of the planned departure. But before he could learn the result, he had to leave. On May 2, he traveled to Copenhagen to speak with Danish explorers who had returned from Greenland about the state of the ice. They had explored the island's southeast coast and had given Nansen accurate maps of the area. Then he sailed for Scotland by way of London. The

Samuel Johannesen Balto and Ole Nielsen Ravna on the way to Greenland

others sailed from Norway with the expedition's equipment and supplies on May 3. On May 9, in Scotland, the reunited group boarded a steamer bound for Iceland. From there, on the evening of June 4, they embarked on the sealer *Jason* and set out into the Denmark Strait for Greenland.

The adventure of their lives was about to begin.

CHAPTER FIVE

An Unexpected Detour

THE *JASON* PLODDED ALONG unhurriedly on a course west, southwest toward the ice fields off eastern Greenland where bladdernose seals would be found. It was a typical sealer, three masted, with a smokestack aft, dependent upon sails and its coal-burning engine: a working ship unused to passengers and cargo. But the ship's crew of sixty-four made space for Nansen and his party with their amphibious boat, gear, and supplies, and tried to accommodate them.

Whatever doubts the sailors may have had about the expedition, the presence of the explorers gave their ship some distinction, and they boasted about it to the crews of other sealers they encountered. Yet their guests did not distract the seamen from the main purpose of their voyage, to earn their livelihood sealing. So when the ship entered the ice fields, it stopped to take seals wherever they were to be found.

The peaks of Greenland became visible in the distance early in June. The *Jason* continued searching for seals on a course southward along the island's eastern coast. But the hunters found fewer seals than they had hoped, and the weeks passed slowly. Nansen, Sverdrup, and Dietrichson joined the hunt and helped take bladdernoses. But Nansen was also pressed into a new and unwanted role. Out of respect for his education, he was often addressed as "Doctor Nansen." The sailors took this to mean that he was a physician and, despite his attempts to explain that he was not, they nevertheless turned to him with their ailments. Nansen found it impossible to avoid listening to complaints about their aches and pains without offending them. So he learned about their digestive disorders, headaches, heartburn, and other physical afflictions, and tried to advise them as best he could.

Nansen often took refuge high above the deck in the crow's nest. From this lookout, he studied the ice-blocked coast, seeking to find a place to land his party. July had arrived, and it was time to go ashore and get started. The *Jason* plowed along offshore just outside a broad band of ice floes. The coastal ice was a menace the sealer had to avoid, or it risked becoming trapped and crushed.

The wide, white belt of ice varied in breadth. At first it was about twenty miles across. Nansen hoped it would narrow as they proceeded, and he watched for this. Then on the morning of July 17, he saw that the barrier ice had narrowed to about ten miles in width and it broke somewhat toward the shore. This, he judged, was about as good a situation as he was likely to find. He expected that his party could make its way through the floes to the coast here in a few hours. So he told the captain that the expedition would disembark.

But crossing ten miles of coastal ice would be risky; conditions change quickly among the drifting floes. Nansen was eager to get going. So he quickly wrote a brief report to a Norwegian newspaper, giving the date and place where he expected to land. Last-minute notes were added to letters to be carried home by the *Jason,* and preparations to depart were hurriedly begun. It soon became apparent, however, that the expedition's boat was dangerously overloaded.

The captain of the *Jason* solved the problem. He gave the

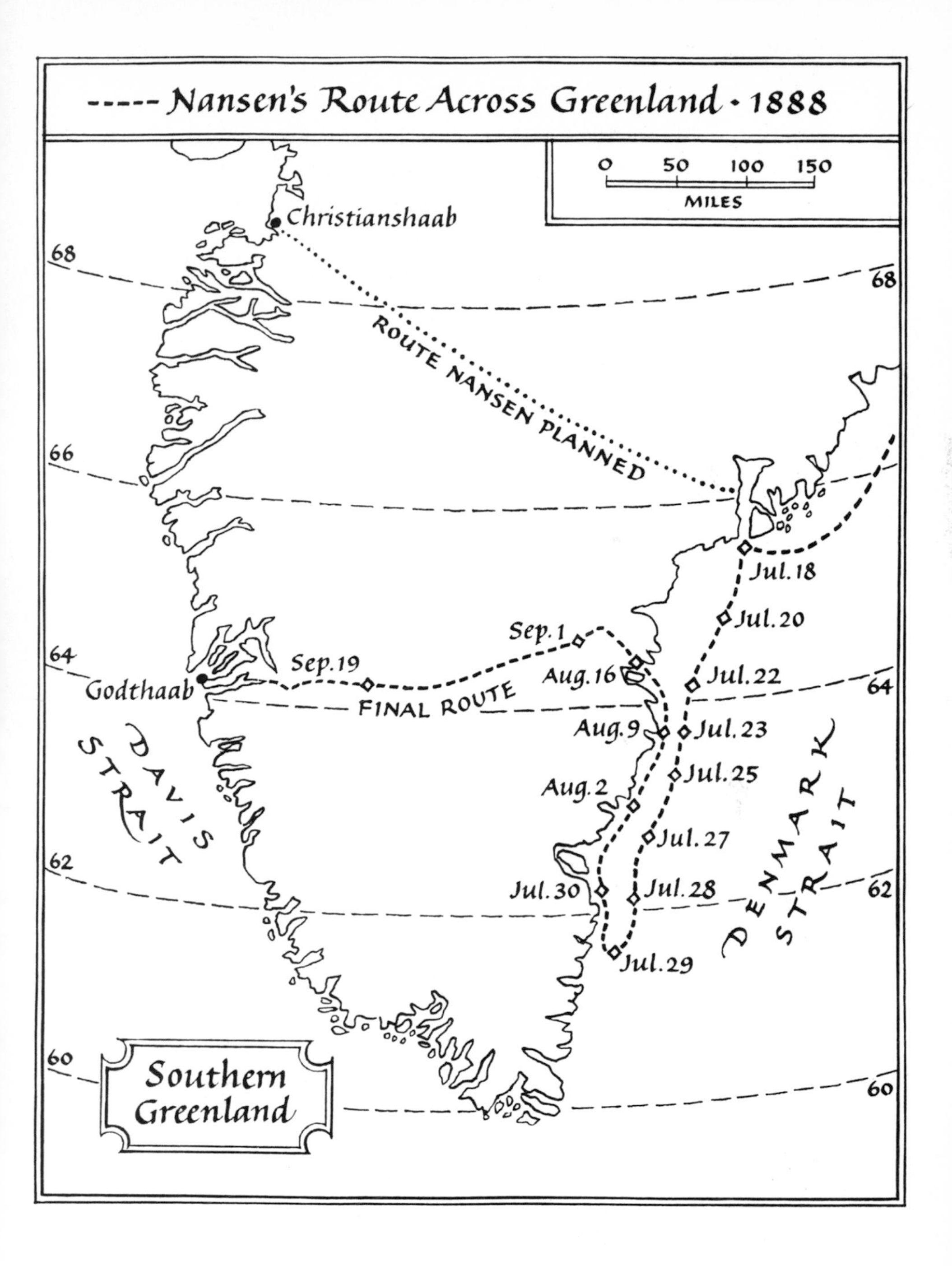
----- Nansen's Route Across Greenland • 1888
0 50 100 150
MILES
Christianshaab
ROUTE NANSEN PLANNED
68
68
66
64
64
62
62
60
60
Jul. 18
Jul. 20
Sep. 1
Sep. 19
Aug. 16
Jul. 22
Godthaab
FINAL ROUTE
Aug. 9
Jul. 23
Jul. 25
Aug. 2
DAVIS STRAIT
DENMARK STRAIT
Jul. 27
Jul. 30
Jul. 28
Jul. 29
Southern Greenland

expedition an additional craft—one of the ship's small sealing boats—and added a quantity of horse meat, a keg of beer, and a chest of bacon and bread. Nansen gratefully accepted the captain's gifts. But the packing and repacking of all the provisions and gear took hours. It was not until seven in the evening that the two craft, each with three men aboard, could be launched. A light rain had begun to fall as the boats, one behind the other, pulled away from the *Jason*.

The expedition was under way at last. Crouched forward in their dark brown, waterproof hooded shrouds, the men pulled at their oars. Ahead lay danger and a world unknown. Behind, fading away in the gloom and chilling rain, was the safety of the ship and all ties to the world they knew. There could be no turning back, for soon the *Jason* would be gone.

Almost immediately, they were in trouble. The drifting floes shifted and closed in around them. Then the edge of a floe cut into the side of one of the boats and threatened to sink it. The men were forced to scramble onto the floe and haul both boats up after them. Despite the freezing rain and the danger, the boat had to be unpacked and repaired. While they worked, however, the floating ice drifted farther out from the shore and joined a larger rapidly moving pack.

To their horror, the men watched helplessly as their floe merged into a dense carpet of ice swiftly streaming farther and farther from their goal. They had become captives of the ice pack and hostages to a current that was quickly sweeping them southward. The rushing floes bumped, collided, and cracked. The rain changed to a drenching downpour. Fortunately, the large floe they were on seemed to be in no immediate danger of breaking up, so, there being nothing else they could do, the men pitched their tent where they were and waited.

After an anxious night during which no one slept, the men took stock of the situation. They were safe for the moment, but marooned on their floe; to leave it would be suicidal.

Their best chance was to ride along for the time being and hope to escape later. Adding to their misery was the fact that during the previous night they had discovered a serious flaw in their "waterproof" tent. The lacing holes that joined the sides, ends, and floor together let the rain in, forcing the men to work constantly to keep puddles from forming. They were thoroughly worn out from their efforts. So they slipped into their sleeping bags to rest. But before Ravna lay down, he caught a glimpse of the *Jason* in the distance and cried out, "What fools we were to leave her to die in this place."

By the morning of July 19, the rain had stopped. With the clearing came the disturbing knowledge that the men were now twice as far from shore as when they had disembarked from the *Jason;* they were also continuing to drift southward. Finally they saw some open channels, packed everything into the boats, and managed to row a distance before it was necessary once again to haul their craft out of the water onto a floe.

The following morning, a new threat appeared. The sounds of crashing waves signaled the danger. Their new floe had broken up during the night and was drifting toward the edge of the pack where breakers were smashing and upsetting the ice. The men scrambled into the boats to flee the tumult. They rowed as fast and as far as they could to find a safer floe. All about them, masses of ice driven by currents were crashing into one another in thundering collisions, gouging bites and causing cracks and fractures to appear. The Lapps were near panic. They jumped into one of the beached boats and huddled at the bottom; Balto comforted the older Ravna and himself by reading aloud from Ravna's Lappish Bible.

The ordeal offshore in the ice pack went on for ten days. The men moved frequently; a large floe might offer them a day, a night, or merely a few hours' safety before conditions forced them to seek refuge elsewhere. But the band of ice in which they were stranded finally drifted in nearer to shore

Anxious Balto sleeps in a boat on Sverdrup's watch

and broke up. The group managed to escape in their boats and make it to the coast. They landed at an offshore island called Kekertarsuak at noon on July 29.

Nansen named the cove they had entered Gamél's Haven, for their benefactor in Denmark. Relieved to be ashore, the group celebrated their survival with a modest feast of biscuits, jam, cheese, and hot chocolate. The cocoa was especially welcome because the men had sustained themselves until then on cold foods, canned provisions, and horse meat.

Glad to be alive and ashore on Greenland at last, the explorers discussed their situation. Almost two weeks had been lost and the brief Arctic summer was waning. But they were about three hundred miles south of the planned position for the east-west crossing. They would have to row back northward before beginning the trek; there was no time to waste. So within hours of their landing, they broke camp and were back on the water once more, navigating the narrow coastal channel.

The men rowed north for days, pausing only for brief

periods to sleep. They stopped on little islands or camped on the barren shore. They took no time to prepare food but lived on short rations of cold biscuits, dried meat, and water.

When small floes blocked their path, they forced their way through using long boat hooks and bamboo poles. They passed fjords, high, rocky cliffs, and glistening glaciers. In places, the men rowed around icy promontories. Sometimes they had to haul their boats out of the water and pull them across the ice. It was exhausting work. Now and then masses of ice would split off from towering glaciers and come thundering down into the sea around them. This spectacle, the calving of icebergs, was majestic and menacing. Awesome, too, was the breakup of the great icebergs. Three times, the men were barely saved from destruction by the disintegration of a nearby berg.

Once the explorers came upon an encampment of Inuit and briefly visited with them. The Inuit women saw that Balto and Ravna used dried sedge grass in their boots and presented them with a goodly supply. The Lapps were delighted and relieved, too, because they had heard rumors before the expedition that the Inuit were cannibals. But the only bloodthirsty creatures the men encountered were mosquitoes. A swarm of these pesky insects attacked them as they slept one night and continued to plague them through a hurried breakfast. Relentlessly, the mosquitoes pursued the group out on the water in the boats until a favorable wind drove them off.

On the evening of August 10, the party arrived at Umivik Fjord. Here, at last, the high, forbidding peaks along the coast had begun to thin somewhat and the mountains were rounded and lower. The men had traveled northward for twelve days and re-covered some two hundred miles, much of the distance lost on their unexpected detour. As the group went ashore, a dense fog settled in around them.

Precious time and supplies had been consumed on their

coastal excursion. But now, at last, they were at a place where they might begin the crossing. Nansen decided they would do so, and this lifted everyone's spirits. Balto, who had kept Ravna's Bible until this time, returned it; he believed he was safe from mortal danger now that he was on land to stay. The expedition's provisions and equipment were quickly unloaded from the boats. Then a fire was started, and everyone shared hot coffee.

Forcing their way through floes

The mist had lifted by morning and the men rose to a beautiful, sunlit day. Across the desolate bay from their campsite, they saw a mountain beyond which they could glimpse the white inland ice. It was necessary to find a path through the coastal mountains to the interior. So Nansen and Sverdrup left Balto, Ravna, and Trana to restore the skis and sleds, and Dietrichson to map the area, while they went ahead to scout out the way.

Satisfied that they had found a route for the expedition, Nansen and Sverdrup returned to camp. But as urgent as it was for the expedition to get started, final preparations for the crossing were not yet completed. The skis and sleds required more work, and boots and other items needed repairs. All the supplies had to be divided and repacked on to the five sleds. These essential tasks took a few more days; when they were done, each sled carried a load of more than two hundred pounds.

Finally the men hauled the empty boats up beyond the tidal high-water mark and positioned them in a crevice in the rocks bottoms-up to form a cairn, a monument, to indicate where they had camped before the crossing. All that seemed unessential for the march was left behind under the boats to lighten their burden. Even something so small as the sail maker's palm was placed in the cache. Nansen wrote a brief history of the expedition thus far, put it in the tin chest that had held their bacon and bread, and added it to the cairn.

At last, on August 15, at 9 P.M., three precious weeks behind schedule, the expedition was ready to depart. The six explorers slipped into their harnesses attached by ropes to their sleds and began to haul them up the coastal ridge. The crossing had begun.

CHAPTER SIX

The White Desert

THE FIRST EVENING of the trek inland started well. The weather was clear and the air brisk and fresh. The frost provided the six explorers with a firmness underfoot, which helped as they made their way in the snow up the barrier mountain. The steepness of the slope, however, forced the men to work in teams to haul the heavily laden sleds, which they pulled in relays until the slope eased. Because of the difficulties hauling, they redistributed the load, removing some goods from four of the sleds and doubling the burden on the fifth; Nansen and Sverdrup pulled that sled together.

The group labored on, each foot hard won. By the time the skies brightened, they had come less than three miles; yet they were too exhausted to continue. They halted, made camp, and wearily slept much of the day. In the evening, they pushed on, trudging through the night again. The weather, by now, had begun to deteriorate and by dawn on August 19 there was a downpour. The men got soaked, despite their rainwear. Finally, the storm became so intense and the visibility so poor that they were forced to stop. The squall lasted for three days, confining the party to its tent. Much of this time, the men slept. They ate only once a day, to save food. To pass the hours, they also wrote in their diaries and told stories; Ravna and Balto read their Bible.

When the rains finally stopped and the men were able to resume the ascent, they found that the downpour had packed the snow, making it easier to progress, except in places where the surface was rifted, steep, and rough. Their shoulders chafed and ached from the ropes they were pulling. Finally, after ascending almost 3,000 feet, they approached the top of the ridge. From this elevation, the group gazed out in awe at the stunning white expanse of the interior ice cap. The smooth, monotonous surface of this vast, white desert to the north and west of them was broken only by rocky peaks jutting up through it. These *nunataks* varied in height and seemed to extend twenty-five to thirty miles inland. It was a strange, desolate, unwelcoming place into which they would trespass. But the team paused to celebrate their progress with extra rations, jam, and biscuits.

Refreshed, the men resumed the ascent once more. There were still rough patches and steep ridges to overcome and, more than once, sleds overturned and had to be righted. But only a hundred or so feet higher, the terrain changed dramatically and the group emerged onto a level, gently rising plain that stretched out in front of them as far as they could see. They had reached the inland ice. Elated, the men ignored their sore, rope-burned shoulders and fatigue and moved out onto the frost-hardened surface.

The going was easier now, especially in the daytime when the sun was out to soften the icy crust beneath them. They were able to make some five, even ten, miles at a stretch except when it snowed heavily and the sleds sank in the fresh drifts. There were other problems, too. The fatless pemmican Nansen had purchased in Copenhagen caused the men to be hungry all the time.

Thirst, too, became a problem. Out on the ice cap, they

relied upon their flasks of snow for water. But in that subzero environment, precious little snow melted even though the flasks were snuggled against their bodies. Nansen and Sverdrup took to sucking moisture from the cherry-wood frame of their snowshoes, all but demolishing their *truger* in this way. Water became so precious that there was none for washing. No one shaved, bathed, or cleaned a dish except to scrape away the crumbs. Nor did anyone scold Balto for polishing the common cooking pan by licking it; germs were of no concern in their frigid camp.

But for all its inhospitableness, the white desert was still a marvel of stunning majesty. At night the moon lit the silent landscape, casting it in a wondrously eerie and unworldly light; it was as if the men were on the moon itself. The skies, too, were magnificent—filled with countless gleaming jewels, and the aurora borealis, the northern lights, put on spectacular and ever-changing displays. Waves of yellow, green, red, and silver radiance swept across the darkness above.

The daytime silence was broken only by the sound of sled runners gliding through the snow, and by the wind. The wind brought snow to the icy plateau. It drove the fine, dry, ice crystals through the men's hooded outerwear to sting them as they plodded along. At night, gusts lashed at their tent, finding each and every loophole in the lacings. Many a morning the men awoke to find their sleeping bags buried under a blanket of snow.

Each three-man sleeping bag had been designed to take the greatest possible advantage of body heat, but it was always the man in the middle who benefited most. The problem with this arrangement, however, was that whenever one man turned in his sleep, the other two had to turn with him. The two bags just barely fit in the tent with room for the cooker, their clothes bags, and a few other items. So the six men routinely had their breakfast of biscuits, liver pâté, pemmican, and a hot beverage, in bed. In fact, they sometimes ate

Crossing the inland ice

their supper there, too, snuggled together to share the warmth. Only their midday meal and snacks were eaten outside on the trail.

The daily marches were monotonous and demanding. Their pace heightened concerns that they might run short of food before they finished the crossing. This fear prodded them on but also made each setback that much more worrisome. Even young Trana, who rarely complained, said, after an especially hard day, "What fools people must be to let themselves in for work like this!"

By August 27 the expedition had progressed along a gradual plane of ascent to an altitude of 6,000 feet—despite blizzards and hills to climb. These adversities put them further and further behind schedule. Their plodding pace, far slower than Nansen had foreseen, confronted the expedition with yet another problem: They would arrive at their destination,

Christianshaab, too late to catch the last ship home before winter set in.

Nansen decided to change his plan. The expedition would turn southward instead and strike out in the direction of Godthaab, another Danish settlement. This route would shorten their journey to the coast. They hoped that they might still be able to find a steamer there before all shipping stopped for the winter. The men were enthusiastic about the new plan. Ravna, especially, was pleased. He had become a constant complainer and was more than eager to return to his Lapland home and his beloved reindeer.

The prevailing winds also added an advantage to the new route, for they blew in the direction the men would travel. Nansen had hoped for an opportunity to use the wind to assist in the crossing. Now that became possible. So the men lashed two sleds together, side by side, to form a sort of snow boat on which they rigged a mast; the canvas tent floor became a sail. The other three sleds were similarly tied to form another craft, and two tarpaulins served as its sail. The tarps, however, could not stand up to the wind, and it took several precious hours of painstaking, bare-handed labor to sew them back together. Finally, after these adjustments were completed, the expedition sailed off on its new course.

But the wind that aided the men was never truly their friend. Its bitter gusts made frostbite a constant threat; all suffered it to some degree. The sun, too, was a danger—causing sunburn and stinging snow blindness. The two Lapps, who had been reluctant at first to use snow goggles, finally consented to do so after painful experiences. What a strange sight the expedition must have been, gliding along on their odd snow boats, weirdly outfitted in snow goggles with their heads wrapped in red silk veils.

When the winds died down again, the men put on snowshoes or skis and resumed pulling the sleds individually. On August 31 they were still ascending the bleak ice plateau when the last of the *nunataks* dropped below the horizon behind them. In honor of their sponsor, they named the rocky peak Gamél's Nunatak. Although reaching it was a measure of their progress, the men felt even more alone now in the midst of this vast, empty sea of white, devoid of all life.

It took them almost two more weeks of grueling effort to climb to the top of the ice plateau, an elevation of some 9,000 feet. Here the surface became relatively flat, but deep newly fallen snow slowed their progress. They were barely able to eke out six miles in the drifts on some days, while on others they might make thirteen. Even on their shorter new course, they fell behind the fifteen to twenty miles per day that Nansen had hoped to achieve when he had planned the crossing, back in Norway.

To ease their hunger and to keep up their energy, the men paused every few hours to eat a cake of meat chocolate. This also helped to break the tedium of the march. Boredom was a menace. It dulled the senses and led to thoughtless error. One absentminded mistake, a brief lapse, could cause crippling frostbite, injury, or damage to the equipment that they all depended upon. Nansen kept a constant watch on the others because it was his duty, as the leader, to bring them all through safely. The men never quarreled with his authority; he shared fully in all the work, usually performing the hardest tasks himself, and listened to their suggestions. They trusted him and followed his orders willingly.

It was Nansen who decided each day when the team had reached its limits and signaled for them to stop. Halting, however, did not mean they could rest immediately. For when they stopped, there were a number of tasks to be done, and they had to be accomplished quickly before the sweat of their exertions turned to ice and froze their clothes to their skin.

In making camp, each man had an assignment: one cleared the ground for the tent, another laid out the canvas floor, and others brought in the sleeping bags, clothes bags, and additional necessities. The cooker had to be assembled, the rations unpacked, and the cooking pots filled with snow. The most difficult chore, however, was setting up the tent itself. The four canvas sides, the floor, poles, ropes, loopholes, and hooks could only be assembled with bare hands; and this meant risking frostbite. Nansen, who had a remarkable endurance to physical pain, nevertheless once described this job as devilish and almost unbearably painful.

Everything done, the men performed one final ritual before entering the tent. Each would stomp about, shaking and brushing his clothes to remove all the snow sticking to them; this was to keep the inside of the tent dry. Once inside, the cooker would be lit to warm their food and to provide heat while the men hastily removed their boots, changed their socks, stripped off their outerwear, and hung it to dry. Ravna and Balto always took care to spread out the sedge grass from their Lapp boots. Each explorer took a turn at cooking, although the supper menu varied little; it was usually soup or stew and a ration of pemmican and biscuits weighed out carefully on a small spring scale and eaten by candlelight.

This was the part of their day to which everyone looked forward. Their exertions over, it was a time for pipe smoking, conversation, and jotting down notes in one's diary. It was a period of camaraderie that drew the men closer together. It was also an opportunity to exchange confidences. Nansen used it to share his future plans with Sverdrup. He told his friend that he hoped to journey next to the North Pole.

In the tent at night, Dietrichson worked on his charts and checked his notes, for it was his special duty to prepare maps of their route and of the areas through which they passed. During the day he would stop regularly to record weather conditions and his observations. This meant handling delicate metal instruments in frigid, subzero winds using his bare fingers. But Dietrichson performed these tasks conscientiously.

The coldest temperatures he recorded were at the top of the ice cap the men were now crossing. Nighttime readings dropped as low as minus 50 degrees Fahrenheit. It was so cold that the explorers awoke some mornings to find their hair and beards stuck to their clothes. It was difficult even to open their mouths to speak. Their clothes and socks froze overnight as stiff as wood. By midday the sun would warm

Preparing supper

the snow, causing it to stick to their socks and boots, forming solid, frozen masses.

In mid-September the expedition came to another milestone. The frigid summit on which they were traveling began to slope downward. At last they were descending from the inland ice cap. Nansen and his party were excited to be beginning the final leg of the crossing. The explorers were eager to catch sight of the coastal cliffs ahead, the landfall that would signal they were near their journey's end.

CHAPTER SEVEN

Leader of the Men with Great Beards

EACH DAY SEEMED TO BRING new signs to encourage the explorers that they were approaching the western coast. Birds appeared; the temperatures grew warmer.

The winds shifted around to trail behind them once more. Nansen had hoped for such breezes to try snow-sailing again. So on the morning of September 19, the men lashed their sleds together in pairs to form two snow boats; the fifth sled had proven too balky to pull and had been discarded. They mounted the sturdy canvas floor of their tent as a sail on one of the craft, using ski poles as spars on the top and bottom to strengthen it. On the other, they made a sail from tarps sewn together and reinforced in a similar way. The squarish sails made the craft look like two small Viking ships on the snow.

Three men crewed each craft. One was positioned out in front of the snow boat on skis; he was the steerer. He controlled a pole attached to both sleds and rigged between them to act as a rudder. The other two skied behind each craft or held on at the rear corners to pole it along when the breeze slackened. The snow boats sailed smartly before the wind. By afternoon, they had covered considerable ground.

Then, suddenly, Balto cried out, "I can see land!" A dark smudge was just visible against the white horizon. Everyone strained to see it through the fine mist of snow that was falling. When the snow subsided, they made out a long ridge of mountains and a smaller peak to the south of it. This was a sight they had all looked forward to, and their spirits soared. Nansen signaled to stop. They would celebrate, even if modestly, on two bits of meat chocolate each.

Soon they were gliding along before the wind again. The day was drawing to a close, but they continued on, eager to make the most of the wind. Nansen was out in front of the lead craft steering when some vague darkness seemed to appear in the

Snow sailing was often dangerous

dim ahead. The gathering dusk made it difficult to see. He sped on toward the shadow, uncertain if it was real.

All at once with a jolt, he realized, to his horror, what the shadow meant. "Crevasse!" his brain must have screamed; he was racing toward disaster. There was no possibility of stopping in time. So he wrenched the rudder to one side and struggled to turn the craft from its fatal path. Desperately, he pulled against the steering pole and fought to save himself and his crew. Bit by bit, the clumsy snow boat began to shift course until finally Nansen managed to divert it; the craft swept past along the rim of the void. Shaken, but safe, he turned immediately to shout a warning to the trailing crew. Now they, too, maneuvered and skidded to safety, avoiding the abyss.

The presence of the crevasse signaled that the expedition had arrived at the border of the western mountains. Alerted by their near accident, the group proceeded more cautiously. They encountered one crevasse after another now until it became much too hazardous for them to risk going on in the darkness. They made camp.

Next morning, September 20, they emerged from their tent to look out upon a glorious scene of snow-covered mountains and deep, dark valleys. Before them lay the whole countryside to the south of Godthaab Fjord. It was an emotional moment for the men who had spent five weeks out on the barren ice. "We were just like children, as we sat and gazed, and followed the lines of the valleys downwards in the vain search for a glimpse of the sea. It was a fine country that lay before us, wild and grand as the western coast of Norway," Nansen wrote.

Now the task was to maneuver around, or over, the perilous clefts that confronted them and to descend from the mountains to the coast below. The snow boats were dismantled; it was easier to manage the sleds separately here. For the next two days, they carefully descended the steep slopes. On

Making their way through a narrow cleft

the evening of the twenty-first, while the others set up camp, Nansen, Sverdrup, and Trana went off to scout the way ahead. The cliff side was so steep that the three tied safety ropes between each other as they inched their way down. Nansen saw a dark patch in the ice below them. When they reached this spot, he found it to be a pond of meltwater. This was the first fresh water they had come upon since starting out on the crossing. "We threw ourselves down, put our lips to the surface and sucked up the water like horses," he wrote.

Next day, the descent resumed. They hauled and carried their sleds, picking their way down around crevasses, across icy ridges, and through drifts of snow. Finally, on September 24, after three hard days, they made it to the foot of the mountains. How delighted they felt to step again on moss, grass, and solid ground and to make camp that evening in a soft field of heather. What a pleasure it was to linger outside their tent around an open campfire sheltered from the frigid blasts and biting cold of the ice cap. Sverdrup filled his pipe with moss and smoked it. Nansen stretched out on a cushion of heather and drifted into dreams. Ravna was comforted, having seen tracks in the heather and abundant grasses; he was happy to know reindeer were about.

Indeed, the North American cousin of the reindeer, the caribou, had grazed these fields for ages. They pastured here in ancient days when the Vikings had settled the land. The Danish colony at Godthaab, to which the party was heading, had been the site of a Viking community some four hundred years earlier. Godthaab lay directly north of a great fjord that now stood between the men and their goal. The safest route to Godthaab was across this long, cold inlet. But they had no boat.

Nansen and Sverdrup decided to construct a coracle, a craft of wickerwork. So they gathered willow branches and wove them into a small, round tub that they covered with canvas from their tent floor; the tent could still be used without the ground cloth. The leftover canvas was cut and sewn between the forked ends of other branches to make paddles. Sewing the sturdy fabric without the benefit of the sail maker's palm, which had been left behind at the start of their trek, was difficult, but Balto and Sverdrup accomplished it. The paddles were then lashed to the ends of ski poles to make two sets of oars. Oarlocks were formed from bent twigs tied to the frame of the coracle.

The men worked quickly all that afternoon of September 27 and, by evening, they had constructed the frail boat. Nansen decided that, because the craft could hold only two, he and Sverdrup would make for Godthaab and send a party back to rescue the rest of the team. This meant taking the flimsy boat out into the deep, frigid inlet and rowing a distance of some fifty-five miles, quite a heroic undertaking. But the two were determined to try it. They took some supplies, a cooking pot, two cups, clothing, a gun, and a camera in the boat and, after a few frustrating attempts to start, they finally departed on September 29.

The two sturdy men, seated one in front of the other, rowed the leaky boat, taking turns about every ten minutes bailing out the bottom with their cups. Nansen soon wished they had built themselves better seats. The makeshift ones they had made from bamboo poles were "the scantiest seats it has ever been my ill luck to sit upon, and I devoutly hope never again to have to go through a similar penance."

For four days they paddled along, rowing and bailing. They saw a group of sea gulls flying about some rocky cliffs and shot several of them. That evening when they camped ashore, they feasted on the gulls. They also stopped along the shore to gorge themselves on tasty black crowberries. Head winds and waves threatened to capsize the coracle one day, but fortunately the great fjord remained calm during most of their passage.

Nansen and Sverdrup landed around midday on October 3 near Godthaab, startling some Inuit there. Then a Danish official came to greet them.

"Are you Englishmen?" the Dane inquired.

"No," Nansen replied, "we are Norwegians."

"May I ask your name?"

"My name is Nansen, and we have just come from the interior."

"Oh," the Dane answered, as if this were a casual, everyday encounter, "allow me to congratulate you on taking your Doctor's degree."

Nansen was so taken aback by the matter-of-factness of the conversation that he nearly burst out laughing. He had just crossed Greenland, the most rigorous and dangerous test of his life, only to be told by the first person he spoke with that he had passed an examination he had taken five months earlier before leaving Norway.

He also learned, however, that the last ship for Europe had

The coracle and Sverdrup

already departed; it was now three hundred miles south on the coast at another port. There was no way for Nansen and his men to overtake the steamer. He was disappointed and also concerned that back in Europe people would think his expedition had failed. Perhaps Inuit in their swift kayaks could carry messages to the vessel before it sailed on, he was told. So Nansen hastily wrote a letter to his benefactor, Gamél, in Copenhagen. An Inuit took the letter and one from Sverdrup to his father and paddled off down the coast. The messages were passed along through a series of relays until finally the last carrier caught the ship. The letters would arrive in Europe a month later.

Nansen and Sverdrup walked the short distance from where they had landed to Godthaab. It was a small settlement consisting only of four or five European houses, a church, and a cluster of Inuit huts, all set in a small valley between two hills. Nansen was welcomed into the home of the Danish superintendent and Sverdrup stayed with the carpenter and boat builder temporarily. Nansen arranged for a rescue party, and it left to pick up the remaining explorers at the far end of the fjord.

The Inuit regarded Nansen and Sverdrup with unusual curiosity. The two Norwegians became known as the strangers who had arrived from the interior in half a boat. Wild rumors had it that these white men had met the mythical creatures of Inuit lore, the great giants of the inland ice and the strange little people who hid in the rocky cliffs that rimmed the fjord. Inuit gathered around Nansen and Sverdrup to stare at them. They called Sverdrup *Akortok,* or "he who steers a ship." Nansen was honored with the name, *Angisorsuak,* which means "the very big one." The expedition was reunited on October 12 and settled down in Godthaab for the winter. Sverdrup and Dietrichson joined Nansen at the home of the local superintendent while the others set up housekeeping in a building.

After the arrival of the entire party, the Inuit gave Nansen the additional title *Umitormiut nalagak,* "leader of the men with great beards." They were fascinated by him and he with them. Nansen admired these durable people who had adapted so completely to life in the Arctic. He hoped they might teach him how to master this harsh environment as they did without the aid of more advanced technologies. So he sought their friendship and help.

The Inuit welcomed Nansen. It was uncommon in their experience to meet a European so eager to learn their ways and their language and so at ease among them. They invited him into their homes, and he lived with them for weeks at a time. The Inuit dug their houses into the earth and built them partly underground using sod and stones. These snug winter burrows resembled giant molehills; to enter, one had to slip down into a hole and crawl through a narrow, underground tunnel to a skin-covered entrance. Here the visitor had to climb up into a chamber where one or sometimes several families lived together. These burrows, primitive compared to the homes of the European settlers, were nonetheless amazingly efficient in conserving heat. Despite subzero temperatures outside, Nansen marveled that the Inuit went about nearly naked inside. Shallow stone lamps of burning seal or walrus fat provided ample heat and light in the dens and were also used for cooking.

Nansen was a humble and respectful guest in the homes of his Inuit friends; he slept as they slept, between animal skins on a raised stone bench. He ate what they ate: raw halibut skin, seal and whale blubber, and fish and meats sometimes raw, sometimes cooked. The foul indoor odors of burning fat, of animal flesh, perspiration, and urine took him some time to get used to, but eventually he was able to ignore them.

As he became more fluent in their tongue, Nansen came to enjoy Inuit stories of seal hunting. He was eager to be taught how to use a kayak and had one built for himself. He was astonished by the light, sealskin-covered craft. Its cockpit was a small hole designed so that the lone hunter's large hooded fur jacket, or *anorak,* formed a waterproof seal with the boat. Should a kayak overturn, its occupant could right it again with his single paddle without taking on water or getting soaked. Nansen practiced until he had mastered the art of kayaking and was able to shoot birds and fish from the craft.

That winter with the Inuit in Godthaab, Nansen learned many new skills for survival in the Arctic. But the courage and humanity of the Inuit also made a deep impression on him. He worried about their future, however, for the colonizers were introducing European ways that threatened age-old, native traditions and upset the Inuits' fragile balance with their environment.

Spring arrived. On April 15, 1889, a steamer finally came to take the expedition home. Nansen, his party, and others from Godthaab excitedly paddled out in kayaks to greet the ship, and it promptly hoisted a Norwegian flag to salute them. The explorers were eager to see their homes again, but Nansen's farewell was not without regret. An Inuit friend told him: "Now you are going back into the great world from which you came to us; you will find much that is new there, and perhaps you will soon forget us. But we shall never forget you."

CHAPTER EIGHT

An Outlandish Idea

THE STEAMER CARRYING NANSEN and his men did not take them directly home but brought them to Copenhagen, where the Danes welcomed the explorers enthusiastically; they celebrated the expedition's achievement for an entire week before the group sailed on to Norway.

Their ship reached Christiania on May 30, a beautiful, clear day. It entered the harbor to the thundering salute of cannons firing salvos of greeting from the ramparts of the great Akershus fortress overlooking the port. A vast flotilla of small boats and craft, tooting horns and sporting flags, sailed out to welcome them. Throngs of cheering people lined the bridges and crowded the wharves to hail the returning explorers.

Nansen, who had been ridiculed for proposing the Greenland expedition only a year earlier, was now acclaimed an honored son by his countrymen; success had turned his critics into admirers. He and his party had become celebrities, and their reception was overwhelming. Above the din, Dietrichson said to Ravna standing next to him on the deck, "Are not all these people a fine sight, Ravna?"

"Yes, it is fine, very fine;—but if they had only been reindeer!" the homesick Lapp replied.

The triumph of the Greenland expedition made an international hero of Nansen. He had defied convention, succeeded despite adversity, and done so in a unique way. Whereas earlier Arctic expeditions had been massive operations requiring numbers of ships and men and great expense, Nansen had shown what a small team with specialized equipment, including skis, could accomplish. He had introduced a new approach to Arctic exploration that was to become known as the "Norwegian Method."

Nansen was also admired in the scientific community, for the Greenland venture had contributed importantly to science. He had revealed the secret of the island's mysterious interior, that the inland ice prevailed throughout and was covered by deep snows that never melted. Nordenskiøld's theory of an oasis was disproved. The expedition had also made a welcome addition to weather research. Dietrichson's painstaking observations suggested that the ice cap had a significant effect on the weather of large parts of the northern hemisphere.

Nansen enjoyed the popularity that the Greenland expedition won him. But even as he savored this esteem, a still-greater ambition stirred within him: the desire to reach the North Pole. For five years he had nurtured this dream of journeying to the Pole. Now the urge grew stronger; he must plan a polar expedition.

But, as it happened, a pretty, dark-haired, young woman reentered his life and captured his attention. Eva Sars, a petite and talented concert singer from a prominent Norwegian family, had met Nansen some time before his Greenland trip. She was a lively, athletic woman and shared his passion for skiing. When they met again, days after his return, Nansen fell deeply in love with her. He delighted in listening to Eva play the piano and sing.

Soon Nansen asked Eva to marry him. People close to the pair said that, even as he proposed to her, he told her he was going to go to the North Pole. So, forewarned, but very much in love, Eva married Nansen on September 6, 1889.

The first weeks of the marriage were rather unusual; for the very next day after their wedding, the couple set out on a lecture tour that would also be their honeymoon. It would

Nansen and his beloved Eva, 1889

earn them an income with which to start their life together. The tour took them to cities all over Europe, to Germany, France, and to England. People were eager to listen to the daring explorer tell about his Greenland adventures; they filled the lecture halls and paid to hear him. Nansen became a polished public speaker. Tall and handsome, he looked like the hero audiences expected; and they were eager to learn what future plans this modern Viking had in store. So he shared with them his hopes for a trip to the Pole.

The lecture tour was a success. When it ended, the Nansens returned home to Christiania. Fridtjof was eager to write about Greenland while his memories were still fresh. Publishing was also essential to his livelihood, for explorers made their income from book earnings as well as lecture fees. Nansen wanted to leave the city and return to the countryside where he could better concentrate on his writing.

So the Nansens moved to a simple, unlived-in house outside the city. It was little more than a shack and was so cold that even drinking water in the pitcher froze. But Fridtjof could write there. He produced most of a two-volume work in this spare place while Eva patiently tried to make do. She wanted a real home, however, so they found a site to their liking in a suburb of Christiania and purchased land. It was a relatively wild and undeveloped tract near where Fridtjof had roamed and hunted wild ducks as a boy. Here they would build a suitable house and make their home.

Nansen took a position at Christiania University as curator of the zoological collection. The job permitted him the opportunity to continue his writing as well as to do research. He was also close enough to his future home to oversee its construction. The place was a handsome cabin constructed from large, brown trunks of pine. Even before it was completed, the Nansens moved in. The house was built in a wood, at the foot of a hill, overlooking Christiania Fjord where the couple had a magnificent view of the ships on their

Godthaab, a home of their own

way to and from the sea. When it was done, the house was named Godthaab (Good Hope), after the refuge where Nansen had spent the winter in Greenland.

Meanwhile he completed his work, *The First Crossing of Greenland,* and illustrated it with photographs he had taken on the journey and with fine sketches he had done. He then began a book about the Inuit people, called *Eskimo Life*. But even as he settled into his new home to write, that restless Viking spirit within gnawed at him. His thoughts kept turning to the North Pole.

The North Pole at the top and the South Pole at the bottom of the world were still unvisited in 1890. Although sailors and explorers had ventured over most of the earth's surface by then, the Poles remained mysterious, missing pieces in the

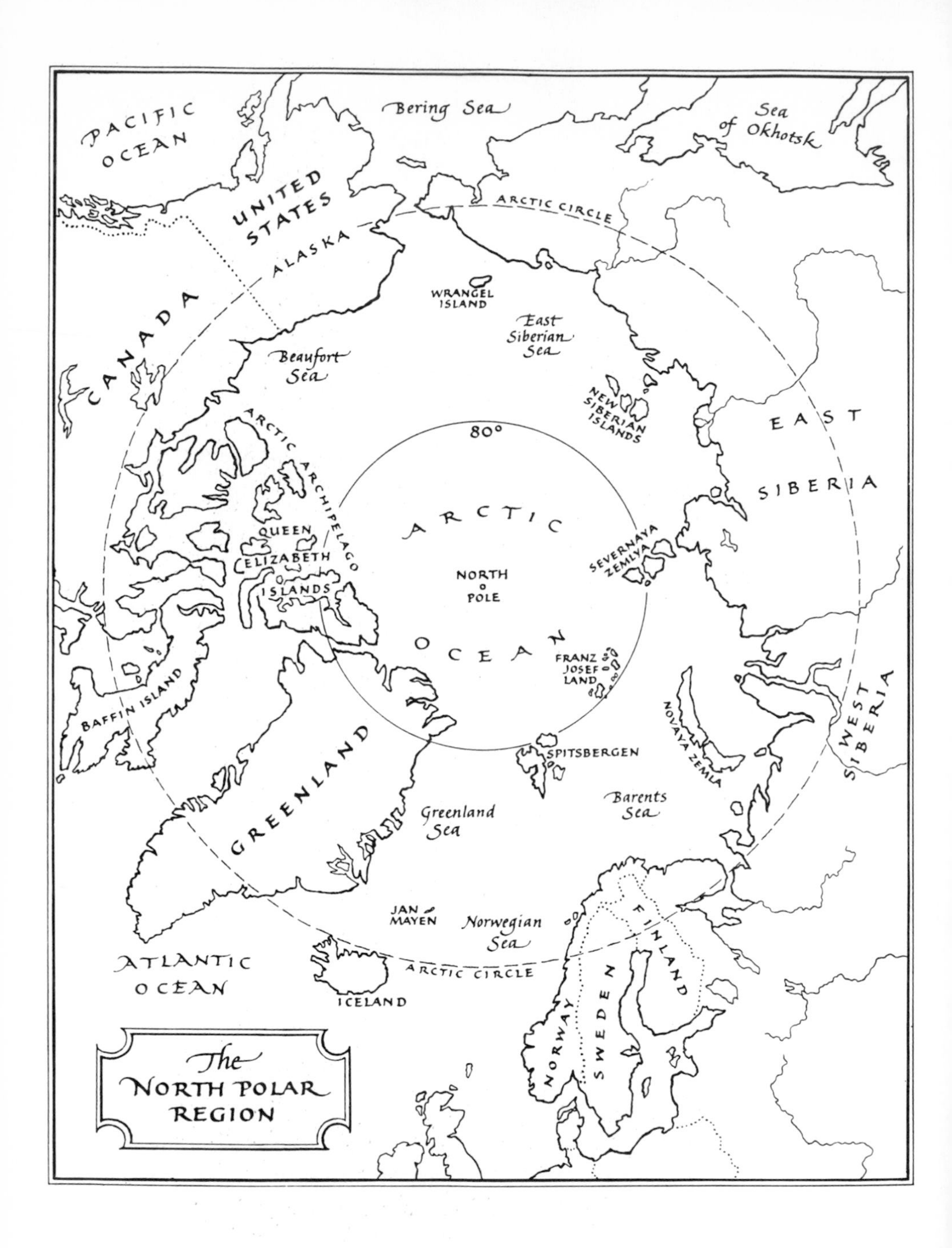

The NORTH POLAR REGION
PACIFIC OCEAN
Bering Sea
Sea of Okhotsk
UNITED STATES
ALASKA
ARCTIC CIRCLE
CANADA
WRANGEL ISLAND
East Siberian Sea
Beaufort Sea
NEW SIBERIAN ISLANDS
80°
EAST SIBERIA
ARCTIC ARCHIPELAGO
QUEEN ELIZABETH ISLANDS
ARCTIC OCEAN
NORTH POLE
SEVERNAYA ZEMLYA
FRANZ JOSEF LAND
BAFFIN ISLAND
NOVAYA ZEMLA
WEST SIBERIA
GREENLAND
SPITSBERGEN
Greenland Sea
Barents Sea
JAN MAYEN
Norwegian Sea
FINLAND
ATLANTIC OCEAN
ARCTIC CIRCLE
ICELAND
NORWAY
SWEDEN

planetary puzzle. No regions defended their secrets more stubbornly. The airplane had yet to come, and the powerful icebreakers and nuclear submarines of the future had not even entered the imagination of those who would probe these remote places. No one yet knew whether the undiscovered Poles were covered by land or water.

Expeditions had tried to penetrate the Arctic ice to reach the North Pole, but the ice defied them; ships were trapped and crushed with the loss of many lives. Those who managed to escape told harrowing tales. The North Pole remained the subject of myth and speculation, but geographers generally believed the area to be a shallow sea with numerous islands.

In the sixteenth century, after the Norse Vikings had disappeared from Greenland and Columbus had opened the Americas to exploration, the great trading nations of Europe, led by the English, French, and later the Dutch, continued the search for a shorter route to the riches of Japan, China, and India. The ocean route southward around Africa was controlled by Portugal and around South America by Spain. So the English and the Dutch sought a northern sea route through the Arctic to sail eastward above Siberia, hoping to find a northeast passage through the ice. When these early efforts failed, the English sent explorers westward into the Canadian Arctic to seek another route, a northwest passage. But this way also proved to be icebound and unnavigable.

Finally the Pole itself attracted attention as a possible route. Many people believed that in the Arctic Ocean, above the frozen coasts of Europe, Asia, North America, and Greenland, there existed an ice-free, open polar sea. They were convinced that one might sail across these northernmost waters to the East.

In 1607, the Englishman Henry Hudson sailed into the frigid waters to seek such a shortcut to the Orient. Hudson left England with a crew of ten and his own son, John. His small ship made its way to a point off northeast Greenland, at 73° north latitude, a place he named Hold with Hope before heavy drift ice halted him. Blocked by the ice, Hudson ventured farther eastward near the island of Spitsbergen and reached a position of 80°23′, farther north than anyone had gone to that time. But this was as far as the ice permitted him to sail.

More than two hundred years later, in 1827, William Edward Parry, another courageous Britisher, thought to cross the Pole by starting off north of Spitsbergen. Parry had read the report of a noted Arctic whaling captain who described this area as having "ice-fields so *smooth* that, had they not been covered with snow, a coach might have been driven many miles over them in a direct north line."

So, expecting to find the Arctic Ocean covered by a surface of flat ice, Parry designed two boat-sleds to travel to the Pole; these had been the inspiration for Nansen's amphibious craft on the Greenland expedition. But conditions were hardly what Parry had anticipated. Ice floes were jammed into irregular heaps that impeded the expedition. Even worse was the movement of the ice, for Parry and his men discovered that, as they trekked northward, the currents were pushing the ice beneath their feet southward. It was as if they were on a great treadmill going nowhere. Parry reached 82°45′ north latitude before he finally turned back in despair; this record would stand for fifty years.

Meanwhile, other brave explorers continued to probe the Arctic. An expedition in 1845 consisting of two well-equipped ships with one hundred twenty-nine men led by the Englishman Sir John Franklin disappeared pursuing a north-west passage in the frigid, icy wilds of northern Canada. Eight years later an American, Elisha Kent Kane, leading one of many parties that had set out to find the lost Franklin expedition, decided to turn northward to search the narrow waterway between Canada's Ellesmere Island and Greenland. Kane, the first American Arctic explorer, also had it in mind to investigate the elusive open sea that might lead to the Pole. Though his mission ended in failure, as he found neither the Franklin men nor the open polar sea, Kane's probe, nevertheless, inspired other explorers and his planned route to the Pole became know as the "American Way."

Nansen studied the history of polar exploration and learned much from the accounts of earlier expeditions. The men who challenged the Arctic braved blinding fogs, icebergs, fierce storms, and temperatures cold enough to freeze the mercury in their thermometers. They faced the ever-present danger of the pack ice and its crushing pressures, forces that could grind a ship to splinters. Nansen could probably imagine the horror of the sailors lying in their bunks, listening to the groans and terrifying squeals of timbers tightening in the grip of the ice. He learned how entrapment in the pack drove men mad and how scurvy, a nutritional deficiency, caused bleeding gums, loose teeth, and disabling weakness.

Two expeditions attracted Nansen's interest the most. The first was the voyage of the *Tegethoff* (1872–1874). This was an attempt, some eighteen years earlier by an Austro-Hungarian team, to find a northeast passage above Siberia. The *Tegethoff* was disabled by severe winds, currents, and ice; frozen in, it drifted helplessly in a northerly direction toward the Pole and came upon a group of uninhabited islands, which the explorers named Franz Josef Land for their emperor. From there, Julius von Payer, one of the expedition's leaders, tried by sled to reach the Pole. He got as far as 82° 5′ north latitude before his provisions dwindled and he was forced to retreat. But Payer thought he had glimpsed land still farther north; he reported this when he rejoined his crewmen, and together they abandoned ship and made their way south on a treacherous journey for nearly three months over the ice to safety.

The other expedition of particular interest to Nansen was that of the ill-fated *Jeannette*. This ship, too, had drifted in a northwesterly direction before its destruction. What struck him was that the ice had carried both luckless ships, the *Tegethoff* and the *Jeannette, toward* the Pole. Could it be that the drift ice was not a barrier after all but a means to reach the top of the world? It might make more sense, he thought, deliberately to enter the frozen pack, instead of trying to avoid it as others had done, and hitchhike a ride to the Pole. The scheme defied all previous polar experience. But would he be able to persuade others that such an outlandish idea could succeed?

Nansen outlined his plan to present to the Geographical Society in Christiania.

CHAPTER NINE

The *Fram*

CHRISTIANIA'S GEOGRAPHICAL SOCIETY met on February 18, 1890 to hear a lecture by their celebrated colleague, Fridtjof Nansen. The recently formed group was probably eager to listen to the explorer reveal his plans for a new expedition to the North Pole.

Nansen began his talk with a brief history of Arctic exploration, pointing out how the ice had defeated all previous attempts to reach the Pole. Then he said something surprising. He spoke of using the ice as an aid to explore the northernmost regions. The polar ice, he explained, almost certainly floats with the current in the Arctic Ocean. If Professor Mohn was correct about the direction of this flow, as Nansen believed him to be, then one should be able to approach the Pole riding upon the drifting ice.

Nansen reviewed the evidence supporting the existence of the north polar current. First, there were the items found in the drift ice on the southwest coast of Greenland that could only have reached there by traveling on a polar current from the site north of Siberia where the ill-fated *Jeannette* had been shipwrecked. These included a schedule of provisions signed by the *Jeannette*'s captain, a list of the *Jeannette*'s boats, a pair of oilskin breeches with the name of one of the ship's seamen on them, and the peak of a sailor's cap.

Another clue was a throwing stick found at Godthaab. This device to hurl bird darts was typical of the kind used to hunt by the native Arctic people living far to the west on the Bering Strait shores of Alaska. Only a current crossing the polar ocean could have carried it to Greenland. So, too, he reasoned, the Siberian logs and driftwood that washed up on Greenland's treeless coasts had to have come on a current flowing through the Arctic seas.

"We cannot escape the conclusion," Nansen continued, "that a current passes across or very near to the Pole into the sea between Greenland and Spitsbergen." If this current could transport massive ice floes laden with debris and timbers from Siberia, he argued, then it could also carry a ship. Such a vessel, he hastened to add, must, of course, be especially designed for this purpose.

The ship he would need, he continued, must be small enough to maneuver between the ice floes so that he could sail northward as far as possible, yet large enough to hold coal and supplies sufficient to last twelve men for five years. The vessel must be strong and shaped to resist great pressure, for he intended deliberately to set her into the ice when he could sail no farther. The ship would then serve as a base for the expedition and would drift with the ice while the team performed scientific observations. Nansen hoped to pass across the Pole from the area north of the New Siberian Islands where the *Jeannette* had been crushed, to the other side of the Arctic Ocean to a point between Spitsbergen and Greenland. There he expected that the ship would escape from the ice and sail home again.

The trip, he estimated, should take about two years. Thus five years' provisions ought to be more than ample. Even so, to prevent scurvy, he would carry a varied supply of foods sealed against dampness in airtight tins. He hoped as well to supplement their supplies by hunting polar bear, seal, and other Arctic animals.

But what if the current upon which so much depended didn't cross the Pole but veered away instead? Even so, Nansen continued, the expedition would not have failed, for it wasn't the exact geographical Pole at 90 degrees north latitude that he was necessarily seeking. He explained, "*Our object is to investigate the great unknown region that surrounds the Pole,* and these investigations will be equally important, from a scientific point of view whether the expedition passes over the polar point itself or at some distance from it."

Nansen's novel plan excited his listeners, and they responded enthusiastically. Professor Mohn, whose theory had inspired the scheme, was particularly gratified. Encouraged, Nansen returned home and began to develop the project further. There were some who were quick to attack his plan, however, pointing out that his proposal depended entirely upon an as-yet unproven theory. It was dangerous, even foolhardy, they contended. But Nansen persevered.

By spring he was far enough along in his plans to begin raising money for the expedition. Once more he turned to the Norwegian parliament for financial support. Now he asked for 200,000 crowns (somewhat more than 1.12 million U.S. dollars today), two-thirds of the amount that he estimated he would need; he would seek the remaining funds from private contributors. But would the government refuse him again?

Three years had passed since the members of parliament had denied Nansen 5,000 crowns for the Greenland expedition. He had succeeded without their support, however, and become a national hero. This time his proposal would cost much more, but the politicians were not about to risk embarrassment again. So they promptly approved his request, but they insisted that the expedition be an all-Norwegian one.

Parliament hoped that one of Norway's citizens would be the first to reach the Pole.

As the project developed, however, it would require more money than Nansen had estimated, and the government would increase its grant. King Oscar II, Sovereign of Norway and Sweden (the countries were united then), would also contribute funds, and private donors would make up the rest. The funds would pay the wages of the expedition's members, provide life insurance for those who were married, purchase provisions, equipment, supplies, and cover other expenses. The biggest cost would go for construction of the ship.

The ship would be specially built to withstand the rigors of its unusual mission. Nansen turned to the best boat builder in Norway. His name was Colin Archer, and he was a Norwegian of Scottish descent. Archer was a robust, fifty-eight-year-old man whose great mustache and long, white beard gave him a biblical appearance. Nansen went to Archer's boat yard located on a bay near the city of Larvik on the coast of Norway some one hundred twenty miles southwest of Christiania.

There the explorer and the boat builder began to design an extraordinary vessel. Nansen, with his mechanically gifted mind, and Archer, with his experience, worked together producing model after model until finally they were satisfied. What they perfected was a replica of a short, broad ship with a thick, smooth, egg-shaped hull; it was rounded from bow to stern (from front to rear) and from the gunwales (the top of the sides) to the keel at the bottom. The ship would not have a graceful appearance; it would look more like a tub. The smooth, round sides would make it difficult for the ice to grip. Pressures would force the floes down under the hull, lifting it, much as a cherry pit is popped when the fruit is squeezed.

Once the overall design was settled, Nansen worked with Archer to incorporate certain other ideas into the plans. On

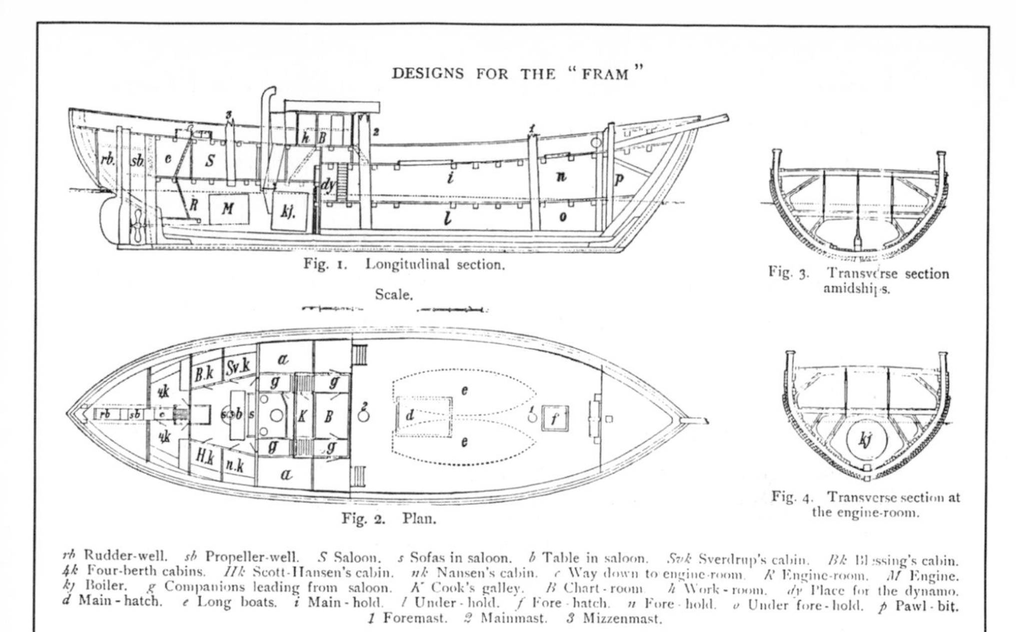

Designs for the Fram.

earlier polar expeditions, the living quarters of the officers and crew were customarily separate. But Nansen's experiences in Greenland had given him a taste of what it might be like for a small group to live together isolated for years from the rest of the world. So he took particular pains to see that the living arrangements on his ship minimized rank and promoted camaraderie. He saw to it that everyone was quartered in the same area and shared a common dining and recreation room.

Archer went on to draft the detailed construction plans and began building the ship. Nansen continued to consult him, but he pursued other matters as well. For the next two years, from the fall of 1890 into the autumn of 1892, while the ship was under construction, he lectured in European cities, accepted various honors and medals for his Greenland achievement, finished his book *Eskimo Life,* and continued his work at the university. But his mind never strayed long from the upcoming expedition.

The ship, meanwhile, grew to be one hundred twenty-eight feet long, about the distance between home plate and second base on a standard baseball diamond, and about a third as wide. The rounded hull resembled a giant coconut, for the bow and stern were identical except for two wells in the stern that housed the rudder and the propeller. The vessel would be rigged as a three-masted schooner with sails, and it would be powered also by a coal-burning steam engine.

Below deck, just to the rear of the mizzenmast, were four tiny cabins for the officers and two larger ones with four berths each for the rest; they surrounded a common room, the saloon. The walls, floor, and ceiling of this entire area were heavily insulated to prevent water from condensing and freezing on them. On previous Arctic vessels, frost often had formed on the cabin walls only to melt in the warmth from a heated stove or reading candle or merely from a breath. The resulting droplets would wet the floor and soak the bed linens, making the berths dank and uncomfortable.

In front of the saloon was the cooking galley, much of it filled by a large, black, cast-iron stove. Over the galley sat a small half deck with a chart room and workroom. The ship's holds, or storage areas, were located below decks in the forward part of the ship. All the coal, equipment, supplies, and provisions the expedition would need would be kept here; there was even space allotted to store rations for sled dogs that Nansen planned to obtain in Siberia.

Much planning went into the ship, for there would be no means to resupply the vessel once it became locked into the Arctic ice. Finally on October 26, 1892, the ship was almost completed and ready to be launched. The stout, sturdy little vessel perched on its frame with its stern toward the water. Three flagpoles stood where the masts would be raised later, two with flags; the center staff was bare, ready to display the banner that would reveal the ship's name which had been kept a secret until then.

The day was crisp and clear, near perfect for the event. Thousands of people had come to observe the launching. The spectators were eager to see Nansen and pleased to participate in what they hoped would be a historic occasion. Nansen mounted the small platform that had been erected beside the ship's bow. Eva followed. Then, clutching a bottle of champagne, she stepped forward and smashed it against the ship, announcing for all to hear: "She shall be called *Fram*." A long, red pennant was run up the empty flagpole with the white letters of the word *FRAM* spread across it. The term *Fram* means "forward" in Norwegian. It had become Nansen's motto on the Greenland crossing. When the brief ceremony was done, the ship was released to slide down into the

The launching: Eva christens the Fram

bay accompanied by the booming sounds of guns and cheers.

Nansen lingered on the launching platform staring after his ship with tears in his eyes. He was choked with emotion, but his face revealed none of it. According to a newspaper account, in his "serene, unembarrassed, steadfast glance, there was no trace of doubt or anxiety."

The final steps to prepare the ship for sea began. Nansen, meanwhile, traveled to London to present his plans for the expedition in a lecture before the Royal Geographical Society. The British organization was old and prestigious and among its members were prominent authorities, including some of the world's most famous Arctic explorers. On the evening of the lecture, the meeting hall was jammed with people eager to hear the young Norwegian.

The audience listened attentively to Nansen, who spoke perfect English. But the evening proved much more trying than he had anticipated. He was challenged by a stream of questioners. Few notables who were present supported him. Admiral Leopold M'Clintock, a renowned expert on Arctic sledding, doubted that the *Fram* would ever be seen again ". . . once she had given herself over to the pitiless polar ice." He predicted that the vessel would likely be crushed in the winter when the pressures of the pack are greatest. Admiral Sir George Nares, another veteran Arctic explorer, attacked Nansen for having no safe line of retreat. Still another critic asserted that there was land surrounding the Pole that would surely obstruct the *Fram*.

Nansen defended his plan. He doubted that land existed at the Pole. But he might have wished to hear the views of Frederick Jackson on this issue. He had met Jackson once and knew, in fact, that the Britisher was planning an expedition in the near future to Franz Josef Land to see whether that recently discovered group of islands extended to the Pole. But Jackson was either absent or silent that evening.

Authorities in other places were critical of Nansen, too,

some insultingly so. Even before Nansen had appeared at the Royal Geographical Society, an American explorer, General Adolphus Greely, had attacked his qualifications for polar exploration. Greely had led a tragic Arctic expedition in 1881–1884 that had cost the lives of most of his party. He was a bitter man who disparaged Nansen and belittled his Greenland experience. "Arctic exploration is sufficiently credited with rashness and danger . . . without bearing the burden of Dr. Nansen's illogical scheme of self-destruction," Greely wrote.

Five days after his lecture at the Royal Geographical Society, Nansen's admirers held a private farewell party in his honor at London's Savage Club. During the dinner, Nansen rose and, as if to show that his critics had not discouraged him, he boldly wrote his name and the date, November 19, 1892, on the wall behind him and jokingly vowed to return to add the date when he would reach the Pole. His friends were delighted by the gesture and later placed glass over the autograph to preserve it.

On his way home, Nansen stopped in Copenhagen to order pemmican again. This time he made absolutely certain that there would be enough fat in it. In Norway once more, he gathered books, games, and musical instruments to take along aboard ship. He collected an accordion and a harmonium, a keyboard instrument resembling an organ that can be played by hand or operated by turning a crank.

Finally the time came to select his crew. Nansen's plans were known to involve great risk but, nevertheless, he received applications from people around the world eager to join him. Not all were enthusiastic, however; one came from a Frenchwoman who confided that she was "tired of life."

Otto Sverdrup, Nansen's trusted friend, signed on to be his captain. He chose a naval lieutenant, Sigurd Scott-Hansen, and a physician, Henrik Blessing, to be his other officers. He also selected eight more Norwegian crewmen, most of whom

The Fram *outfitted for sea*

had experience at sea. They came with varied backgrounds. F. Hjalmar Johansen, a round-faced, short, sturdy man and a lieutenant in the army reserve, was, for example, a champion gymnast. Another man—whose special experience, it was hoped, wouldn't be needed—had been a head keeper in an insane asylum. Most of the men were married and had families. Nansen was among these fathers. On January 8, 1893, Eva had given birth to a daughter, Liv.

The *Fram* was finally fitted out for sea. Its three thick, wooden masts were set in place with sails and all their rigging. The ship's engine was installed. But what was really remarkable in the workings of the ship was the addition of a dynamo, a generator. The *Fram* was one of the first Norwegian vessels to have electric lights.

Nansen had the hull of the *Fram* painted gray, the gunwales green, and the half deck red. He chose these colors for their brightness, anticipating the dark months ahead. These and other details filled his mind as the time of departure neared. He would lie awake at night, trying to think of all the needs that might arise during the voyage, and he would often light a candle so that he could jot something down. Eva, tired herself perhaps from tending to little Liv, complained about this.

But Nansen tried to prepare thoroughly, for he knew full well that the cruel polar sea did not welcome visitors and it had no mercy.

CHAPTER TEN

Ice Blink, Water Sky

PEOPLE GATHERED ALONG THE WHARF that rims Christiania harbor below the old stone fortress, Akershus Castle, on the morning of June 24, 1893. They kept coming, despite the overcast skies, until a sizable crowd had collected; for it was known that the *Fram* was sailing this day, and folks wanted to see her off on what they hoped would be a historic voyage.

A short distance out in the harbor, still more spectators lined the rails of gaily decorated boats to watch as well-wishers trooped on and off the stout ship. Puffs of smoke rose from her single smokestack aft to signal that the engine had started and the crew was ready to sail. But 11 A.M., the scheduled departure time, came and passed. Fridtjof Nansen had not yet arrived.

The onlookers stirred as the *Fram*'s motor launch approached and edged up to the ship. Everyone was anxious to catch a glimpse of Nansen as he boarded with his black-and-white dog, Kvik; she was a sturdy working dog brought to him from Greenland. The excitement of the crowd did not seem to affect him. On deck now, the handsome thirty-two-year-old leader of the expedition appeared calm and deeply serious.

Earlier, in the privacy of his home, Fridtjof had said good-bye to his beloved Eva and to their daughter, Liv. The parting had been difficult, all the more painful because the couple knew that it might be their final farewell. Nansen would long remember this parting and the sight of little six-month-old Liv innocently clapping her hands in the cabin's window as he left Godthaab. "What would I not have given at that moment to be able to turn back," he wrote in his diary.

With Nansen's arrival, the last visitors left the *Fram* and he gave orders to raise anchor and get under way. Just past noon, the ship's bow swung around and the *Fram* steamed out into the harbor. The crowds on shore waved their hats and handkerchiefs and cheered, and a flotilla of boats bearing friends trailed in the wake of the departing ship. Some launches carried bands and serenaded the *Fram* with rousing patriotic songs. Well-wishers chanted, "Long live our Nansen!"

It was a stirring send-off, but Nansen's attention was focused on shore. He stood before the chart room on the ship's bridge, peering intently through a telescope for one last glimpse of his home as the *Fram* made her way toward the sea. The sun broke through the murk for an instant, and in that brief moment he found Godthaab. There standing beside a bench, under a fir tree, was Eva waving bravely. Nansen's spirits leaped, but the sight of her also revived the pain of their parting. The weather seemed to turn with his mood; for the gray, overcast sky resumed and it began to rain.

Next day, at noon, the *Fram* reached her birthplace and put in at Colin Archer's boat yard where she took aboard two longboats that were positioned on the foredeck above the main hatch. The boats were large enough to hold the entire crew in an emergency. She also took on four lifeboats that were lashed to her sides. Besides the new additions, the *Fram* carried a motor launch and a small fishing pram.

By late afternoon the following day, the ship was ready to leave. Nansen's brothers had come to see him off. They joined Archer and a friend for a short sail on the departing vessel. Archer's affection for the *Fram* was so apparent that he was invited to take the wheel and steer her. He was proud to guide "his child" a short distance on her first voyage. Then came final handshakes and good-byes; the visitors left in a small boat, and Archer shouted one last farewell. The *Fram* responded, saluting her maker with the first firing of her guns.

The ship made her way out into the coastal waters toward the southern tip of Norway. This first leg of the journey was quite pleasant. The weather improved and the waters, sheltered by the landmass from the North Sea, were calm. For two days the crew took advantage of the easy sailing to become better acquainted with one another and with their vessel. Twenty-five-year-old Scott-Hansen was acting captain in the absence of Sverdrup, who was to come aboard later en route. The naval officer and Nansen had much to discuss because Scott-Hansen would be responsible for the scientific observations of the expedition. They chatted in the small chart room long into the evening of June 27 as the *Fram* rounded the southern tip of Norway, left protected waters, and turned west, northwest into the North Sea. Outside on the foredeck down in front of them, the ship's cook slept peacefully in one of the longboats; the covered craft was a comfortable place to nap on deck and had already acquired the nickname "Grand Hotel."

The North Sea into which the *Fram* was proceeding has a deserved reputation as one of the most fitful bodies of water on earth. As the ship plowed on, the sea grew choppy and rougher; the *Fram* rose and fell on ever-increasing waves. Then, all at once, the full force of a storm struck.

Nansen and the young naval officer were deep in conversation and caught off guard when suddenly the chart room door burst in like an open floodgate and admitted a blast of seawater, drenching them. The deck below them was awash. The *Fram* was instantly in the deadly grip of a gale. Nansen promptly became seasick. He had felt nauseated often on the *Viking* eleven years earlier. Now he stood outside on the bridge desperately holding on, spewing his supper.

Water broke over the bow of the *Fram* and poured over her rails. The sea tore cargo loose. Casks, poles, and timbers rolled free and tumbled about the deck crashing into the rails and threatening to smash the struts that held the longboats. The commotion roused the sleeping cook. He jumped from the Grand Hotel and scampered to safety, clutching his clothes under his arm. Then out he came again to rescue his sea chest. Water swept over him, threatening to wash him overboard, but he stubbornly held on to his possession and made his way below.

Meanwhile the rest of the crew came up to wrestle with the loose cargo—dangerous work on the slippery, pitching deck. It took about an hour, a harrowing eternity, to secure everything once more. But many casks and timbers were lost or jettisoned into the sea.

The *Fram* survived the brief ordeal, and much was learned from the trial. The ship had not been designed for rough waters but rather to withstand the pressures of the Arctic pack. She was expected to have difficulty in heavy seas, and now her weakness was clear. In a storm, Nansen wrote, the *Fram* "rolled like a log."

The vessel moved on, and fair weather returned. The *Fram* put in briefly to Bergen where Nansen enjoyed seeing friends again. Then it was back to sea, as the ship continued northward under clear, radiant skies.

The *Fram* proceeded up the scenic channel between the majestic mountains of the mainland coast to starboard, on

Calling at Bergen on the journey north

her right side, and the almost-continuous chain of hilly offshore islands and rocky islets to port, on her left. The splendor of this passage with gleaming streams cascading down steep slopes and countless seabirds swarming in shadowed valleys on either side must have cheered the sailors.

So, too, the men of the expedition must have felt encouraged by the children and grown-ups who came to the shore to wave and shout greetings to them. Fishermen in small boats paused to look up from their poles and nets at the oddly shaped ship and called to the explorers. Even passing steamships crowded with passengers hooted their horns, dipped their flags, or fired cannons in their honor. All along the seaside, Norwegians in villages and towns were eager to express their pride and support to the crew of the *Fram*.

At a village near the city of Trondheim, Sverdrup joined the ship. The *Fram* also took aboard medical supplies there. At other stops she loaded quantities of dried fish, food for the dogs the expedition would acquire later. The vessel steamed on, crossed the Arctic Circle, and continued uneventfully northward. She had entered the land of the midnight sun, where in spring and summer daylight prevailed twenty-four hours around the clock.

On July 12, the *Fram* arrived at the sealing port of Tromsø and was welcomed by a severe summer storm with driving snow, sleet, and chilling winds. There additional supplies, coal and Arctic-weather clothes were taken on. The ship also unexpectedly acquired another crewman, an experienced Arctic seaman. He would be the thirteenth member of the expedition. But if any of the men felt superstitious about this, none gave a hint.

Out at sea again, the *Fram* rounded the North Cape, the northernmost point of the European continent, and called at Vardø, a small island port off the extreme northeast coast of Norway. From there, she headed east into the Barents Sea off the northern coast of Russia. Almost immediately the vessel entered heavy fog. Dense mists are common to these frigid waters in summer, and the *Fram* was wrapped in fog here for the next four days. Then the mists cleared briefly, allowing Nansen to see the south island of a pair of mountainous Russian islands known as Novaya Zemlya (New Land). But then the fog dropped to blind the ship once more.

Navigating in dense mist is always difficult for ships at sea, but in Arctic waters it can be a nightmare. Nansen had not expected heavy ice conditions in these Russian waters so early in the season; the sea here is still usually clear in late July. But ahead, hidden in the vapors, ice drifted silently toward the *Fram*. The first hint of trouble came when strips of ice began to pass around the bow. Then suddenly, massive floes confronted the vessel.

Sverdrup scrambled up the mainmast, disappearing in the dim above. From the crow's nest overhead, he bellowed orders to the helmsman below: "Hard astarboard!" "Hard aport!" "Steady!" "Hard astarboard again!" The helmsman pulled at the wheel, forcing the ship to turn and twist to avoid the great floes. Finally, after weaving a zigzag course through the maze of ice without sustaining damage, the *Fram* broke out into clear waters again near the coast.

Nansen was relieved, too, that the ship had proven to be agile and highly maneuverable. She could pivot and turn "like a ball on a platter," he boasted. The *Fram* won this first battle with her foe, but he was concerned that meeting such heavy ice so early could hint of worse problems ahead.

The *Fram* made for the Yugor Strait, a narrow passage between the west Siberian coast and an offshore island. Nansen had arranged for a sloop bearing coal to meet the ship there with additional supplies. The sloop, however, had not yet arrived when the *Fram* dropped anchor off a small coastal hamlet to wait for it. Nansen went ashore to the meager settlement of tents and a few houses. Here, also by plan, he was to obtain sled dogs for the expedition from a trader.

The trader's agent, it would turn out, was a man named Trontheim whose father had been Norwegian. Trontheim had thirty-four yelping Siberian huskies for Nansen. The agent took him for a wild, hair-raising test drive through the countryside on a sled pulled by ten of them. Even more remarkable was the fact that the spirited dogs had towed the two hefty men and the sled over the bare, dry ground.

Days passed with no sign of the coal sloop. The men went ashore to meet Russian traders and local Samoyeds (known today as Nentsi), nomadic reindeer herdsmen, with seal, bear, and reindeer skins to exchange for flour, sugar, tea, and other items. The Russians and Samoyeds were invited aboard the *Fram*. Trontheim was a frequent dinner guest. His observations of shipboard life would later appear in a Russian newspaper. What impressed him was the lack of rank and privilege among the crew: no distinction "being made between the common sailor or captain, or even the chief of the expedition. The doctor, too, takes his share in the general work."

While they waited, the men serviced the ship's engine and boiler and Nansen took off with Sverdrup and another crew member in the launch to scout the route ahead. They motored eastward, stopping here and there to hunt, and bagged geese, ducks, and one or two snowy owls. The tundra, the plains of low-lying Arctic vegetation, abounded with tiny, colorful flowers and Nansen stooped to gather some blooms. When they had traveled about twenty-eight miles, they went ashore again to climb a ridge for a view of the Kara Sea beyond.

The Kara is carpeted with ice most of the year. Dense floes covered the sea then. But Nansen knew from charts Nordenskiøld had given him that the Swedish explorer had found a clear path between the ice and the coast on his journey through the Northeast Passage fifteen years earlier. Sure enough, there it was, and the channel was just wide enough for the *Fram* to pass. Delighted, Nansen returned to the ship.

Time continued to pass with still no sight of the coal sloop. This confronted Nansen with a problem. To delay any longer was to risk that ice conditions would worsen and even block the open channel that remained for them. But could they do without the additional coal on which he had planned? They would have to, he decided; it was urgent that they go on. The crew wrote letters to their loved ones; Nansen pressed the tundra flowers he had collected between the pages of his message to Eva. Dispatches and the letters went ashore, and the *Fram* weighed anchor about midnight on August 3.

The ship had sailed only a short distance when dense fog forced her to halt for a few hours. The crew, waiting for the mists to lift, was entertained by a chorus of howl-

Nansen in his cabin, with a portrait of Eva and Liv behind him

ing, barking dogs tied up on the foredeck unused to the roll of the vessel. But soon the *Fram* moved on eastward into the Kara Sea. She continued hugging the broken coastline for three weeks, keeping between the fixed ice seaward and the shore.

Progress was slowed by stiff head winds and drifting ice; the ship had to maneuver frequently to avoid colliding with meandering floes. Nansen's experience aboard the *Viking* now proved useful. The sealers had taught him to observe the skies to search out clear waters. Dark blue heavens, or "water sky," ahead signaled that the way beyond was open and free of ice.

The *Fram* steamed on, passing islands, one of which the crew named for their captain. Near some islands off the coast, they stopped to refit the boiler, which had begun to act up, and to hunt reindeer and bear. Then on August 28, they encountered dead water. Dead water is a layer of fresh water floating on the surface of the denser ocean like a great saltless tear. This unusual obstacle clings sluggishly to a vessel, creating drag and slowing it. The burdensome dead water stuck to the *Fram* for days into early September when some thin ice chanced along to shear it away.

The delay had been costly, for the summer was waning quickly. When the *Fram* reached Cape Chelyuskin, the northernmost tip of the Asian continent, heavy ice conditions were already awaiting her. Nansen worried that the ice might force the expedition to winter over here on the Siberian coast. But then a storm arrived and broke the ice free from its grip on the land, creating a coastal channel around the cape for the ship to pass. Nansen, from high in the crow's nest, guided the vessel. At four o'clock in the morning on September 10, the *Fram* rounded the infamous cape, marking a significant milestone on her journey. Despite the hour, Nansen ordered the flags to be raised and the ship's guns fired. Then he passed out cigars and threw a party with harmonium music, fruit, and punch for all in the saloon. "*Skoal* [good health], my lads," he toasted them, "and be glad we've passed Chelyuskin!"

Beyond the cape is a stretch of the Siberian coast where several rivers empty into the Arctic sea, usually keeping it free of ice. Here at the mouth of the Olenek river, Nansen had planned to stop to obtain more dogs. But the lateness of the season prompted him to pass up this opportunity in favor of pushing on farther east to the New Siberian Islands. Here, too, he had planned a stop to check on depots of provisions he had arranged for in the event of an emergency. Again, however, he chose instead to take advantage of currently favorable conditions and sail by.

Now the *Fram* changed course and turned north, steaming into seas where no other ship had ever sailed. The skies ahead gave no sign of "ice blink," no hint of ice below. The ship was headed toward the Pole, and the way seemed clear. Was there, despite Nansen's doubts, an open polar sea, as the early Arctic explorers had hoped, after all? Sverdrup thought so.

The question was answered by a rude jolt that shook the *Fram* the following day. Nansen scrambled up on deck to see "the edge of the ice, long and compact, shining through the fog." The ship had bumped against the fringe of the great Arctic drift ice. Nansen changed course to cruise along the rim of the ice pack in a northwesterly direction, seeking to edge still closer to the Pole. But by September 22, the ice halted further progress north, and they moored the ship to a large floe drifting in the open water.

They paused now to observe conditions, to shift the remaining coal stores, and to service their troublesome boiler once again. They had another problem, too: lice. While they stopped, the crew declared war on this pesky enemy. The pests had apparently come aboard weeks before when they had entertained guests in the Yugor Strait.

Determined to be rid of the lice, the crew decided to exterminate them with steam. So they attached a hose to the boiler and steam-cleaned the cushions and mattresses where the stowaways had hidden. Then they packed all their lice-infested clothes and underwear into a large barrel, sealed it tightly, and pumped in steam through a hole. After weeks of itching and scratching, the crew would have its revenge by scalding the bugs to death. In their zeal, however, they miscalculated. They forced so much steam into the barrel that it exploded, blasting their long johns and clothes all over the deck.

Meanwhile, the ice gradually closed in and encircled the ship. On September 25, Nansen recorded, "Frozen in faster and faster! . . . Winter is coming now." At about 78°50′ north latitude, 134° east longitude, the *Fram* became icebound. The lives of all on board soon would depend upon the accuracy of her design and whether, indeed, there was a north polar current.

The expedition's fate was sealed.

CHAPTER ELEVEN

Icebound

THE *FRAM* SAT DEAD STILL in the fast-closing ice pack. Aboard, the men of the expedition sprang into action to change her over from an ocean-going vessel into an Arctic research station; the lowering sun and the chill winds of autumn prodded them on.

The crew hauled up the ship's rudder to prevent the ice from damaging it. They dismantled the engine, stored it away, and installed a workshop in its place. Some of the men drained the boiler while others set up a carpentry shop in the hold and a tinsmith's in the chart room. The sailors arranged space on deck for a blacksmith; later the smithy, with its fiery forge, would be moved onto the ice for safety. Other activities, from sail making to shoemaking, were performed in cabins or in the saloon.

Nansen was pleased with the transformation. The ship was securely lodged in the drift ice ready to begin the polar drift, and she was self-sufficient; she had to be, alone and cut off now from the rest of the world. But Nansen was confident. "There was nothing from the most delicate instruments down to wooden shoes and axe-handles that could not be made on board the *Fram*," he wrote.

The days grew cooler and the sun traveled ever lower in the sky. The temperature dropped to minus 11 degrees Fahrenheit early in October. With the engine no longer driving the dynamo to produce electricity, the men relied on dim oil lamps to light their dark, windowless cabins and the saloon. So, eager to restore power, they set about assembling a windmill on the port side of the foredeck. It would take weeks of tinkering before the great, sweeping canvas sails of the mill would turn the dynamo properly and produce current for the lights again.

Meanwhile, the scientific work of the expedition began. Detailed weather observations were conducted every four hours around the clock. Scott-Hansen was in charge of this work, and he was assisted by Johansen, whose services as the

Nansen reading the temperature of a water sample

ship's stoker were no longer needed with the boiler drained and the engine down. Johansen's new job was to record data from thermometers, barometers, and wind gauges set up in different parts of the ship and out on the ice. At night the man standing watch performed certain of these duties.

Scott-Hansen and Johansen also made astronomical observations. These were done every other day if the weather was clear. The crew was particularly interested in this work because the data was used to determine the *Fram*'s position. It was common to find a number of men waiting outside Scott-Hansen's cabin around noon on days after the sightings to learn the results of his calculations; their spirits rose or sank depending on the ship's progress in the drift.

Nansen's special interest was the polar sea itself. He lowered water collectors and thermometers through a hole in the ice to measure the salt content and temperature of the water. He investigated the currents, made depth soundings, lowered nets, and dredged the sea bottom to collect samples of creatures. He also studied the colorful aurora borealis for indications of electrical activity in the Arctic skies. After a time, Blessing, the ship's doctor, assumed responsibility for this work.

Blessing was the only one aboard the *Fram* with little to do in his own field. Occasionally, he was called upon to ease a backache or to treat a minor intestinal complaint, but the crew was basically healthy. Once a month, nevertheless, Blessing would weigh and examine each member of the expedition and collect a sample of blood to study. The men, always concerned about scurvy, welcomed this attention. Blessing, however, never found any sign of it. But he did make an awful discovery: the body lice were back.

It was essential to eliminate the parasites before they got into the men's warm winter furs or these, too, would become infested. But how? Steam wasn't available with the boiler drained. They would have to rely on mother nature this time.

So everyone removed their affected clothes, cabin rugs, and other infested things and placed them out on the frigid deck. The fragile pests froze; the expedition was finally rid of them.

The crew also adjusted to the new experience of living icebound in the Arctic. It must have seemed strange at first not to hear the familiar rumble of the engine down below and the sounds of water lapping against the hull; the pitch and roll of the vessel were missing, too. But the men grew accustomed to these changes and settled into a new routine.

The crew rose each morning at eight o'clock and ate bread, muffins, cheese, cured meats, and fish together at a long table in the saloon. After breakfast, they worked. They carried on scientific projects, built equipment, and performed chores: washing the decks, keeping the sails and rigging in good repair, hauling up provisions from the hold for the cook, and

The crew ate together at a long table

gathering fresh-water ice from the floes to melt for drinking, cooking, and washing. Every day a hole had to be opened anew in the ice for access to water should a fire occur; this hole was also used to make the depth soundings. The dogs required attention, too. They needed to be taken out on the ice and also fed their rations of dried fish and biscuits.

At one o'clock, the men reassembled in the saloon for their main meal of soup, fish, meat, potatoes, macaroni, canned vegetables, desserts, and beer while it lasted. After dinner, some members of the crew took a short nap; others preferred to smoke and talk in the galley. Then it was back to work until six, at which time the men ate supper, a meal similar to breakfast. A quiet time to look at pictures or to read followed; the *Fram* had an excellent library that featured histories of earlier Arctic explorers, accounts of Parry, Franklin, Kane, M'Clintock, Payer, and others.

The saloon, the center for all leisure activities, was a small, narrow, low-ceilinged room with a skylight. The walls were painted white for brightness and were so thoroughly insulated that the area was comfortably dry. The widest part of the room butted against the galley. The men dined here seated before a long table on a couch. More seating was arranged around the thick base of the mizzenmast that pierced the center of the room. Paintings of Norwegian scenes, the harmonium, and a stove to provide warmth helped to make the saloon more homelike and cozy.

At about 8 P.M., the quiet period ended and the men played chess, checkers, dominoes, and a game called *halma* similar to Chinese Checkers. Card games, however, were most popular, and the crew would bet their bread rations on a good hand. Some nights there was music and they sang. Johansen played the accordion and others might join him on the flute, violin, and harmonium. They mostly played and sang Norwegian songs, but one of Johansen's favorites was the American tune "Oh, Susanna."

Entertaining themselves aboard the Fram. *From the left, crewmen Nordahl, Blessing, and Johansen*

The crew turned in about midnight after the watch had been arranged. Each man stood watch for an hour, during which he was responsible for the safety of the ship and was required to write up his diary. The person on watch also had an additional chore. Whenever it was time for the weather observations, he had to read the instruments and record the data. No one enjoyed this task; it meant venturing out onto the ice to the thermometer house in the subzero cold, and there was always danger of polar bears lurking nearby. The man on watch listened carefully to the dogs, whose barking might give them warning of bears.

Although they are more aloof and less aggressive than North American grizzlies, polar bears can also be dangerous to human intruders, especially when they are accompanied by their young or are very hungry. The bears would cause some excitement for the expedition. The first incident occurred on the afternoon of October 2. Scott-Hansen, Blessing, and Johansen were out on the ice setting up a tent to make magnetic observations. As the three worked, a large polar bear meandered into view not far away.

Hoping that the bear hadn't seen them, Blessing started to tiptoe back toward the *Fram* to get help. But he hadn't gone far before the bear began stalking him. Blessing retreated to the tent, expecting somehow that the three men together might be able to scare the animal away. But the bear headed straight toward them. Then Scott-Hansen remembered a trick he'd read about in a book. He pulled himself up as tall as he could, stepped out boldly in front of the oncoming bear, waved his arms violently, and bellowed at the top of his lungs. His companions followed his example, making a loud,

First encounter with a polar bear

raucous chorus. But the bear, unimpressed, still charged them.

With only moments to spare, the desperate men seized what tools they could and bolted for the ship screaming "Bear! Bear!" No man can outrun a polar bear on the ice, however, and the trio would certainly have been caught but for a stroke of luck. The bear was curious; it stopped to investigate the tent and paused to sniff and poke about. By this time, Nansen had heard the commotion and had come down onto the ice with his rifle. As the bear turned to pursue the men again, Nansen killed it with one well-aimed shot.

The expedition's usual routine resumed. But conditions changed quickly as winter approached. The crew observed that just north of the *Fram* the drift ice was becoming increasingly jammed. Ice floes, driven by winds, tides, and currents, were beginning to collide. They watched the masses crash together with frightening impact, heaving great chunks of ice up and over one another. Long, irregular walls of ice and snow, pressure ridges, and small mountains formed; these ridges and hummocks rose twenty or more feet in the air, about the height of a two-story building.

Then on the afternoon of October 9, following dinner, the men were startled when suddenly the whole ship trembled and they heard unearthly screeches and loud rumbles. They fled the saloon and rushed up on deck to see what was happening. The crushing force of the pack was squeezing the hull on all sides. Ice pressure was testing the ship. Would the pack crush the *Fram* in its icy grip as it had so many vessels before? Each crew member must have prayed that the *Fram* could withstand the force as the pack pushed against the ship hour after terrifying hour.

But the ice, pressing on the rounded hull, was repeatedly forced down under it, thrusting the vessel upward. At times, the *Fram* lifted several feet into the air before breaking the ice beneath her and settling again. All afternoon and on into evening, the struggle continued. Finally it eased and calm returned for a brief period. Then the force of the ice built up once more to test the *Fram* over and over again for several days. But the sturdy ship met the challenge. Nansen described what this was like in his diary on October 13:

> Now we are in the very midst of what the prophets would have us dread so much. The ice is pressing and packing round us with a noise like thunder. It is piling itself up into long walls, and heaps high enough to reach a good way up the *Fram*'s rigging; in fact, it is trying its very utmost to grind the *Fram* into powder. But here we sit quite tranquil, not even going up to look at all the hurly-burly, but just chatting and laughing as usual.

Finally the packing eased. The crew's confidence in the *Fram* soared as a result of her performance. They were cheery even as the lowering sun dropped below the horizon on October 26, bringing on the long, dark night of Arctic winter. It helped their morale, too, that the windmill was finally functioning to provide them with glorious electric light once more.

Nansen wondered where the *Fram* would be when the sun returned. He worried about the ship's progress. Its path was irregular, ranging first to the north and then straying southward again. Six weeks into the drift, on November 7, she was farther south than where she had started. The prevailing winds were having a far greater effect on her course than Nansen had anticipated. He felt discouraged by her plodding, zigzag roaming and began to have doubts. Was his theory of a north-going current valid? Troubled that he might well have risked the lives of his good crew on an errant mission, he withdrew and shared his thoughts with no one. He turned the problem over in his mind, searching for answers. But each time he reviewed the matter, he came to the same conclusion. The evidence, especially the Siberian driftwood that washed up on the shores of southwest Greenland, told him that his theory had to be right; he just knew it.

CHAPTER TWELVE

Darkness and Danger

WEEKS OF DARKNESS AND COLD slipped by with temperatures as low as minus 22 degrees Fahrenheit. New problems arose which concerned the dogs. The animals had been removed from confining kennels on deck and placed out on the ice nearby to give them greater freedom. But the dogs began to fight. One would attack another and, if the victim was severely wounded, the rest would join in to tear the injured dog to pieces. Four huskies were killed. So in November, Nansen ordered that a crewman watch the dogs during the day and that they be returned to their kennels on deck at night.

The animals, however, weren't entirely safe on board either, as it turned out. A marauding bear managed to climb aboard the *Fram* three times one evening and make off on each occasion with a dog. Of the thirty-four huskies obtained in Siberia, disease, dog fights, and bears had claimed eight already. Then Nansen's dog, Kvik, remedied matters. When it became evident that she was pregnant, a warm, fur-lined, borning box was set up for her below decks. There, on the thirteenth of December, she presented the thirteen men of the crew with thirteen pups. The pups would remain indoors until early spring when they would be allowed to roam the deck and, still later, to romp on the ice with Kvik. Of the litter, however, only four would survive to become strong, healthy dogs.

In December, despite some further meandering, the ship moved northward again to about the same latitude where the drift had begun. At last the *Fram* was progressing, if slowly, in the right direction. Nansen brightened. Regardless of the darkness, bitter winds, and temperatures ranging down to minus 40 degrees Fahrenheit, he left the ship to hike out over the pack. On one moonlit night in January 1894, he found the ice before him stretching out into a broad, flat plain and thought it splendid for sledding. The flat surface inspired the thought of making a sled trip to the Pole.

He wrote this idea in his diary, confiding that, although he still expected to stay with the *Fram* and pursue his original plan, he might reconsider. "[I]f it takes us in the wrong direction then there is nothing for it but to try the other."

To Nansen's dismay, the *Fram* wandered once again. He was frustrated, too, by unexpected problems with his scientific work. Before the voyage he had accepted the commonly held view that the polar sea was shallow. So he had brought along only some six thousand feet of sounding line, thinking it ample. But now the steel wire failed to reach bottom; the ocean was deeper than he had thought. Finally, after struggling with the bothersome problem for a while, he improvised a solution. He and others laid out one of the ship's cables on the ice, separated its strands, and spliced them together end to end to make additional line for the soundings. It was not easy work, handling steel wire in bitter, subzero temperatures, but they got the job done.

The depth Nansen ultimately measured was greater than twelve thousand feet. This discovery led him to another insight. The extreme depth of the polar sea was probably the

Lowering the sounding line to measure the sea depth

reason why the northward current lacked force. In the shallower body that he had envisioned, the current would likely have had greater strength driving the ice and the *Fram*, despite the head winds. Indeed it was discouraging that by February 18, the *Fram* had traveled only one degree northward, merely sixty miles or so, to the eightieth degree of latitude, and that had taken five months. At this dawdling pace, it might take eight years to complete the voyage.

In an effort to combat monotony, the crew had taken to celebrating birthdays, holidays, nautical milestones, and all manner of events, real or contrived. A party was planned, for example, on February 20, the date the sun was to reappear. But when the day arrived, clouds hid the sun from view. The crew celebrated anyway with rifle fire and a four-course dinner. All this feasting, and their ordinarily generous rations, had, by now, produced many a double chin and potbelly.

The tedium was especially terrible for Nansen, who daydreamed often about home and family. "What I would not give for a single day of struggle—for even a moment of danger!" he wrote at the end of March. But boredom wasn't the only cause of his discontent. It appeared to him now that the fitful course of the *Fram* would likely carry her below the Pole. Although the main purpose of his mission was to conduct scientific research in these northern regions, he had cherished the hope of reaching the Pole.

At times, when he felt lowest, it seemed to him that his life was lacking direction. He yearned to find purpose. So achieving the Pole had, perhaps, special meaning to him. He would not give up the dream easily. Once again he considered making the journey by sled. His excursions out on the ice on skis or by dogsled became more purposeful; he sought to learn when conditions might be most favorable and decided that April would be the best month for the trek. Later, as spring progressed, rising temperatures brought dense fogs; the ice softened and winds caused the pack to break up, creating open channels, or "leads."

In mid-July the men built six sturdy double kayaks to add to their emergency equipment. Nansen himself constructed a one-man kayak in August. It was similar to one that the Inuit in Greenland had taught him to use. He secretly thought of taking it along if he made a dash to the Pole, for such a trip would probably require some travel over water. Meanwhile the *Fram* continued in a northwesterly direction. By September, Nansen had concluded that, as the ship tracked to the north, its progress should accelerate; the voyage would likely be completed, after all, closer to the time he had originally estimated. But he felt even more certain now that the *Fram* would not cross the Pole. He would have to leave the ship to reach that goal.

Although back in Norway Nansen had not planned to trek on foot to the Pole, the challenge of such an adventure excited him. He was sure that he could assemble whatever he might need for such a journey from the stores on board the *Fram*. On November 16, he confided the scheme to Sverdrup.

Nansen proposed to depart the following spring, 1895, when daylight reappeared, but no later than March. Timing would be crucial because the trip to the Pole and back to land should be completed before the summer melt made travel over the ice too difficult. Because the *Fram* would continue to drift in his absence, he would not attempt to find her again but would make for Novaya Zemlya or Spitsbergen where, he hoped, he would find a sealer to take him home. Nansen would take one companion on the polar trek; two men would have a better chance of succeeding than one alone.

Whom to choose? Whoever it was would be risking his life. Sverdrup wanted to go, but he understood that, as captain, he had to remain with the *Fram* and bring the ship and her crew back safely to Norway. Nor could Scott-Hansen leave; he was needed to continue the scientific research. Blessing could not go, either: the ship should not be left without a doctor. Everyone on board was likely to volunteer, but Nansen decided that Johansen would be the best choice. Johansen was a strong, able skier with proven endurance, and he was an agreeable companion.

Nansen talked to the former gymnast. He warned Johansen that the trip would be dangerous and that he should consider the matter carefully. But Johansen was so eager to go that he jumped at the offer. The rest of the men were told next. As Nansen had expected, each of them would have volunteered, had he asked.

Nansen and the others began to prepare for the journey. They built a second kayak for Johansen. Nansen designed the boats so that they would fit on the dogsleds when the men were traveling over ice. The crew set about to make the sleds, skis, tent, sleeping bags, and other items the team would need. From the ship's stores, they assembled a small camping stove, tools, guns, a medical kit, camera, and additional equipment and supplies. They packed pemmican and gathered other dried foodstuffs for the journey.

Science and a bit of whimsy: Scott-Hansen's observatory

Meanwhile the crew continued to perform their normal work and made ready for a second winter in the ice. They raised a canvas awning over the foredeck as a shield against the wind. Scott-Hansen replaced the tent where he made magnetic observations with a more substantial snow hut. When the igloo was completed, the scientist set up a scarecrow on its roof for the fun of it. December winds came, howling across the ice, rattling the ship's rigging and bringing snow. On December 13 the *Fram* reached 82° 30′ north latitude, setting a new record. She had come the farthest north of any vessel thus far. This was reason enough for another shipboard celebration.

From the start, this second winter of the drift seemed more severe than the first. The temperatures dipped lower and the winds caused ice pressures worse than those before. At times the packing sounded like volleys of cannon fire. On New Year's Day the *Fram* was violently jolted by the jamming ice.

Two days later, on January 3, Nansen awoke in the morning to another roaring din. This time a massive pressure ridge appeared off the port side of the ship. The immense wall of ice advanced toward the *Fram,* pushing a huge floe before it.

The weight of the floe depressed the ice in which the *Fram* was embedded, causing the ship to lean toward the approaching mass. Although the *Fram* was able to withstand the usual pressures of the pack, the vessel's tilt presented a new danger. If the *Fram* did not break free and right herself before the ridge arrived, she could be buried beneath it.

Nansen believed that the *Fram* would survive, but he prudently ordered that preparations be made to abandon ship if necessary. So the crew began to off-load provisions and equipment onto the starboard ice. That evening, however, a crack developed which forced the men to move the supplies

A pressure ridge threatens the Fram

to a still-safer location. The parting ice also caused water to rise and flood kennels that had been built on the ice. It became necessary to move the dogs back onto the deck. The men hauled additional supplies and food up from the hold so they could readily be shifted onto the ice. Finally the weary crew turned in, leaving the anxious man on watch to observe the approaching menace.

That night and all next day, the threatening ridge pressed ever closer. It nudged to within ten feet of the *Fram*. Still it came, slowly, relentlessly. "This is like dying by inches," Nansen thought. The following day, January 5, the pressure ridge reached the rail of the *Fram*. Nansen was awakened by "a thundering and crashing outside in the ice, as if doomsday had come." Preparations to leave the ship hastened. By 8 o'clock that evening, ice and snow towering six feet above the rail amidships began to crash down onto the vessel, crushing the canvas awning on the foredeck.

Now came the command the crew dreaded. "All hands on deck!" Nansen called. He ordered the men to clear the saloon and the cabins of their things and to leave the ship. Poor Sverdrup, who was about to take one final bath in a tin tub in the galley, was stark naked and obliged to hurry into his clothes.

Nansen set the dogs free, and they scampered down the gangway onto the ice. The crew followed. The men gathered out on the moonlit floe. They shouted excitedly to make themselves heard above the booming racket. Then the pounding eased and all was quiet; the packing had stopped. After a while, the men reboarded the *Fram,* ate, and went to sleep. They took the precaution, however, of sleeping in their clothes this time and leaving all doors open. But the ordeal was over. The *Fram* had broken the grip of the ice and raised herself. For the time being, the men were secure. All that remained of the incident was the heavy work of chopping away the ice and snow that had tumbled onto the ship and

Clearing ice from the Fram *after a pressure ridge*

covered the port side of the vessel. This toilsome chore would take days.

Slowly life aboard the ship returned to normal, and preparations for Nansen's trek to the Pole resumed. He and Johansen tested their equipment and practiced with their new skis and sleds. They took lessons in first aid from Blessing. The two slept out on the ice to test their sleeping bags and found them uncomfortably cold. So Nansen had a single, two-man bag made. It was sewn from thicker reindeer hide and was warmer because it held the body heat of more than one person.

Nansen estimated how much food the two men would take on the trek. Because there was no possibility of resupply or rescue, and they could not carry sufficient provisions to complete the trip, he would have to rely eventually on hunting bears, birds, and seals to survive. So the amount of ammunition they should take became an important concern. Once they left the *Fram,* the two of them would be totally on their own on the barren ice.

This was the kind of challenge that had always attracted Nansen with his passion for danger. Would the trek to the Pole be his final adventure?

CHAPTER THIRTEEN

Alone on the Frozen Polar Sea

NANSEN AND JOHANSEN ASSEMBLED their dog teams, bid farewell to the crew, and struck out over the ice, northward, on March 14, 1895. The *Fram* was fast in the ice at 84°4′ north latitude, 102° east longitude, some three hundred fifty-six miles from the Pole. Twice before, they had been forced to turn back because of problems with their sleds, but this time the tiny expedition, two men, twenty-eight dogs, and three sleds, vanished quickly in the vast, white expanse.

They traveled single file, Nansen with Kvik leading the first sled, followed close behind by Johansen with the other two. The sleds were laden with equipment, including the two kayaks and provisions; each was pulled by a team of nine huskies. Because it was not possible to carry sufficient food for the whole journey, especially enough to feed the dogs, the grim law of survival would require that, as they progressed, the weakest animals would have to be sacrificed in order to feed the remainder. Both men accepted this brutal necessity, but it would prove difficult. They knew also that their own provisions would last but a hundred days. By then, they must reach some place to hunt and replenish their food supply or perish themselves.

Undaunted, the two explorers were determined to reach the Pole. The surface of the drift ice they crossed was rough, and the going was difficult. The choppy, uneven ice upset and overturned the sleds repeatedly. They encountered pressure ridges over which they had to lift and carry the sleds, impeding their progress. But then, after a few days of struggling, the ice leveled out into a relatively smooth plane and they found travel easier. They advanced seven, nine, even fourteen miles a day, slowed only by leads; these open lanes of water required them to make time-consuming detours.

Time was a crucial element in their race to the Pole and back, for each delay increased the odds against them. Travel conditions would only worsen as the warmer months approached, and their supplies were limited. Yet there was nothing to be done but to cope with each obstacle as it arose and carry on. Minor mishaps were common. One day, for example, a jagged bit of ice ripped into a sack of fish meal, spilling the irreplaceable flour. A valuable hour was lost while the men scooped up the precious meal and repaired the

Nansen, second from right, and Johansen, fourth from left, departing for the Pole.

bag. On another occasion, rough ice damaged their odometer. It cost hours to fix the instrument that they depended upon to measure the distances they traveled; then it broke off altogether and was lost for good. Nansen could only estimate their progress after that.

The dogs, too, caused minor delays. They frequently tumbled and jumped over one another as they ran, causing their harness ropes to tangle. At least once every hour or two, the expedition had to stop to free the dogs' knotted traces. This was bothersome, especially because it could only be done bare-handed and the air temperature was minus 40 degrees Fahrenheit.

But the ice conditions remained favorable and the weather clear and sunny. Nansen was optimistic. In his diary on March 20, he enthused, "If this goes on the whole thing will be done in no time." Indeed it looked that way, for on the twenty-second, they did a record twenty-one miles. In little more than a week, they had advanced up into the eighty-fifth degree of latitude.

On the next day, however, the smooth ice that had favored them once more gave way to a rough, broken surface, and awesome pressure ridges and numerous hummocks rose in their path. Making headway became arduous. The men shouted and drove the straining dogs forward. Again and again, Nansen and Johansen had to push, lift, and pull the sleds over horrific barriers. They also encountered leads once more and were forced into wide, looping routes to get around them. Nansen frequently went on ahead of the tiny troop to scout out these detours; this meant that he often traversed the same path three times over.

Johansen's tasks were no less demanding. Managing two sleds and teams in these rigorous circumstances without coming to grief required skill, strength, and endurance. Each man labored all day and on into the sunlit, Arctic night. "Sometimes," Nansen wrote, "we were so sleepy in the evenings that our eyes shut and we fell asleep as we went along. My head would drop, and I would be awakened by suddenly falling forward on my snow shoes [skis]."

When, finally, their exhausted bodies could go no farther, the men would find a place to camp out of the wind, if possible, against the sheltering wall of a pressure ridge. Johansen would feed the worn and hungry dogs and secure them for the night. The dogs were fed only once a day, at night, after the day's march was done. Meanwhile, Nansen would pitch their two-man tent, gather ice to melt for fresh water, start supper, and unpack whatever they might need, including their next day's breakfast. It usually took about an hour to melt the ice and to heat their meal. So while they waited, the two would crawl, shivering, teeth chattering, into their "dear" bag to warm themselves and to thaw their frozen clothes.

Their strenuous exertions produced bodily moisture that settled into their clothing during the day and froze, causing the woolen garments to stiffen. The clothes became brittle shells that "crackled" and felt like "suits of ice-armor." The rigid garments also rubbed against their skin as they marched. Nansen developed painful sores on his wrists from this chafing and wore bandages to protect himself. When the men rested, the warmth of their sleeping bag thawed their clothes, now making them damp and soggy. All they had, however, were the things they wore, so they slept and marched in the same clothes.

Footwear was another matter. Nansen had learned the value of the soft, light Lapp *finnesko* on his Greenland expedition, so both men wore them now. But these reindeer-fur boots had to be turned inside out and worn that way to dry each night. The sedge grass used to line them also had to be dried; so the two would spread the grass over their chests and legs while they slept and then carefully repack it into their boots each morning.

Food consisted of a stew of pemmican and potatoes called *lobscouse* or a mixture of powdered fish, cornmeal, and butter, *fiskegratin,* or just soup with pemmican and bread. The men were sometimes so weary that they fell asleep while waiting for their supper to warm. But their slumber wasn't always peaceful, for in his sleep, Johansen would often relive the day's march and shout out to the dogs, "Get on, you devil you! Go on, you brutes!"

Their morning routine varied little. They awakened, ate breakfast in their bag, wrote in their diaries, and then made ready to resume the trek. The tent would be folded, the sleds repacked, and the dogs harnessed. Repairs to their clothes or gear that might be required would be done at this time, and Nansen would make navigational observations to determine their position. The explorers' lives settled into a regular pattern: they marched, ate, slept, and made ready to march again.

All the while, nature seemed to challenge their intrusion, confronting them with one terrible obstacle after another. Conditions on the ice kept worsening. Craggy, all-but-impassable ridges and gaping leads obstructed them. Each punishing mile was a struggle, and the ice before them looked even more dreadful. Nansen's earlier optimism faded. On April 3, for example, he noted in his diary that even from their current location, the journey back to the nearest land would be three times farther than the distance they had come. He worried about the conditions that might confront them when they attempted their return.

Another unpleasant surprise jolted the explorers the next day when Nansen determined their position at 86° north latitude. Despite their grueling efforts, they had come a shorter distance north than he had estimated. The Pole was still two hundred and forty miles beyond them.

Nansen's doubts deepened. So many obstacles loomed in their path, and precious time was passing. Already it had been necessary to destroy two of the dogs, and he realized that he had needed more of them from the start. For this, he blamed himself. Now he regretted passing up, in his haste, the opportunity to obtain additional huskies at the Olenek River on the Siberian coast. "What would I not give to have the Olenek dogs?" he complained.

Notwithstanding all this, the disheartening truth was that, as he and Johansen fought to make their way north toward the Pole, the winds and currents were driving the ice under their feet southward. They were marching on the same giant treadmill of drift ice that had stopped explorer William Parry some sixty-eight years earlier. Nansen's notes in his diary for the next few days showed his discouragement:

> I begin to think more and more that we ought to turn back . . . The ice grew worse and worse . . . when we stopped this morning I had almost decided to turn back . . . We hardly made four miles yesterday. Lanes, ridges, and endless moraine of ice-blocks; and this continual lifting of the sledges over every irregularity is enough to tire out giants . . . I am rapidly coming to the conclusion that we are not doing any good here.

By April 8, the men had advanced one hundred and thirty miles over the polar drift ice to 86°14′ north latitude. They had established a new record in Arctic exploration, having come farther north than any other humans had ventured to that time. Because they had nowhere encountered land, doubt was cast on the popular notion that the top of the world was surrounded by land. But they were still two hundred and twenty-six miles from their goal.

Ever the realist, Nansen was forced to accept that their chances of reaching the Pole were nil; to continue the effort would be futile and suicidal. The time had come to surrender his cherished dream. It must have been difficult. All his life he had accomplished what he had set out to do, but this time his will and determination would not prevail. The Pole was not to be the achievement of his life. He would have to discover other purposes to give his days meaning.

That night, alone on the desolate icescape, Nansen and Johansen huddled in their tiny tent and accepted their disappointment. Tucked in the shelter of a protecting ridge in minus 25.6 degrees Fahrenheit, they marked the end of their polar pilgrimage, dining on lobscouse and celebrating with bits of chocolate. They planted two Norwegian flags that they had hoped to place at the Pole in the snow outside their tent and turned in. The next day the journey homeward would begin. They would proceed over the ice pack to Franz Josef Land from where they might sail to Spitsbergen and meet a sealer.

The first weeks of the trek south were easier; the ice became more level and passable. They made such good progress that they lengthened their marches. Perhaps because of the fatigue this produced, both men accidentally allowed

Farthest north, 86°40′ north latitude

their watches to unwind and stop. When they discovered this, they estimated how much time had elapsed and wound them up again. But from then on, they could never be certain of their position; to calculate their longitude accurately, the location east or west, they would have required the precise time. Because there was nothing to be done about this, Nansen would rely on his best guess and they pushed on.

One day, on the trek southward, the explorers observed a dark object in the otherwise-monotonous, white environment around them. It turned out to be the huge trunk of a tree that had become lodged in the ice and had drifted with it. They dearly wished to cut it up for firewood but could not remove it. So they carved their initials and their approximate latitude, 85°30′ north, on the trunk and left it there.

May arrived. The temperatures moderated and the breezes blew stronger. The winds caused the ice to crack and part. Leads opened, obstructing their path, forcing them to take time-consuming detours around them. To make matters worse, the rising temperatures turned the surface snow and ice to slush, and the dogs and sleds sank in it. By the middle of the month, with only twelve animals left, it became necessary to discard one sled and to divide the dogs between the remaining two.

Travel on the ice would only grow worse as temperatures continued to climb. Soon the kayaks, lashed to the sleds, would be needed, but they were full of holes and damaged from repeated accidents. Nansen decided not to stop to repair them just yet but to push on as long as it was possible to make headway. So the expedition trudged on. It struggled through heavy snowstorms, circled pools of meltwater, and detoured around leads. These open channels were becoming more numerous and ever wider. One day, a school of narwhals—small, toothed whales—surfaced in one of the lanes.

The drudging retreat put a severe strain on the men and dogs. By the end of May, the expedition had dwindled still further. Only eight huskies were left. Even Kvik, weakened from overwork, had been sacrificed. The temperature continued to rise, climbing above the freezing point. The drift ice was melting and splitting into separate, floating islands. Nansen and Johansen put on waterproof boots now to cope with the melt. The expedition was compelled to seek places where the floes met so it could cross over from one to another. Progress was slow and cautious lest the floes shift apart and separate the two teams of dogs and sleds.

The men had withdrawn now to a position 82°30′ north, a latitude visited by earlier expeditions. Yet despite using a map made by the respected explorer Payer, showing islands in the region, they still saw no hint of Franz Josef Land. They were lost; they knew neither where they were nor when their journey might end. Nansen, aware that their provisions might not last too much longer, was eager to press on. But with conditions on the ice deteriorating, he was forced to stop and to repair the kayaks. In early June, with water sky reflected in the distant clouds, he called a halt and the two men spent a precious week patching holes and bracing the weakened frames of their boats.

Rations were cut for the men and the dogs to conserve food. The kayaks were tested and, although they still leaked, they were packed back on the sleds and the march resumed. Hunger now added to the expedition's miseries. One dog was ravenous enough to bite the end off one of Johansen's skis. Still the suffering troop trudged wearily on, towing their burdens through knee-deep slush. They were down to only three huskies now, so the men made themselves harnesses from leftover dog traces and hauled the sleds side by side with the animals. When they met wide leads, the kayaks were lashed together to carry the teams to the next floe.

On June 21 they were paddling between floes in their leaky kayaks feeling discouraged when finally they struck a bit of good luck. A large seal popped up in the channel and lolled

Crossing a lead

near the boats; the men were determined to have it. Johansen slipped his rifle out from his pack, carefully took aim, and shot the seal. Nansen, who had raised a harpoon, plunged it into the animal before it could sink. They happily towed the seal to the next floe.

No banquet could compare in pleasure to the feast that followed. Although seal soup, meat, liver, and blubber might not appeal to everyone, it tasted heavenly to the starving expedition. The seal also provided them with enough food and blubber fuel for a month. They shot another seal, too, but there was a downside to their fortunes as well.

The kayaks had leaked so badly that many of their supplies were wet and some of their ammunition damp. It would be necessary for them to set up camp again to dry things out and to waterproof the boats. In the meantime, they hoped that the channels would continue to widen and become more navigable. So, reprovisioned as they were with seal meat, the men settled in and began to recover from the rigors of the march. They ate their fill of seal and enjoyed such delicacies as pancakes made from seal blood fried in blubber and topped with sugar.

Nansen managed to kill yet another seal. One of the three remaining dogs, however, was so exhausted that it had to be destroyed. But the end of June brought another unpleasant surprise. Nansen's newest observations showed them to be approximately where they had been at the beginning of the month. So, despite weeks of exertion, the shifting winds and currents had all but kept them in place.

Rains came in July, washing away much of the snow and slush on their floes. The men repaired their battered sleds and worked on their leaky boats. Nansen also took time to go hunting, and he killed a bear and its cubs. Now there was bear meat to feast on, and the two ate it for breakfast, dinner, and supper.

By mid-July, the men were almost ready to move on again. They had caulked the boats with an improvised compound of seal oil and crushed crayons that Nansen had brought along for sketching and applied a mixture of carbon soot and seal oil to the shell of the kayaks. They completed the waterproofing with materials—pitch, resin, and other substances—that they had carried from the *Fram*. Finally they discarded everything they could spare to lighten their load and repacked the sleds.

On July 22, after a month in the camp, they picked up the traces and struck out over the ice again with the two remaining dogs, hoping to find Franz Josef Land.

CHAPTER FOURTEEN

The Winter Hut

A DARK SMUDGE APPEARED in the distance, rising at an angle against the boundless, white horizon. Nansen had observed it before in camp, but mists had made it difficult to see even with his telescope. Now on July 23, as the men trekked on, the blemish reappeared, popping in and out of the vapors beyond, but always in the same place, in the direction they were heading. Then the haze lifted, and the explorers could clearly see that it was a ragged line of black, rocky peaks jutting through a cover of snow—a mountainside. Their spirits soared. After almost two years on the frozen Arctic sea, land was at last in sight again and it seemed close, perhaps only a day's march away.

The mountain, in fact, was much farther than they had guessed. It would take thirteen days of hard going to reach land. The two trudged on, cheered to be so close. Each man pulled his sled with one dog to assist him. The ice was choppy and it rained; they labored in sodden clothes.

The dampness affected Nansen badly. He developed a backache so severe that each step pained him. Johansen lent a hand to help pull his sled. When they stopped to rest at

Hauling the kayaks and sleds, Nansen leading

night, Johansen set up camp and had to remove his companion's boots and socks for him. Nansen realized how much each man needed the other. His turn to save Johansen would come soon enough.

In a few days, Nansen recovered and was once more able to haul his own sled. It was hard making headway on the rough ice, but they marched on, advancing as best they could. On August 4 they encountered a lead and needed the kayaks to ferry across. Nansen had just dragged his boat to the edge of the ice when, suddenly, he heard a commotion behind him and a shout: "Take the gun!"

Nansen spun round to find Johansen pinned to the ice, struggling with a she-bear. He jumped to pull his rifle from the kayak. But as he did, the boat slipped from his grasp and slid into the water. Now he had to haul the kayak back onto the ice to get the gun. Meanwhile Johansen fought for his life. He pushed against the bear's powerful neck to keep it from biting him. Though he was muscular and extremely strong, Johansen was no match for the beast. "Now you have to hurry or it might get too late!" he called frantically.

The bear, however, wearied of the struggle and pulled off Johansen to lunge instead at one of the huskies. By this time, Nansen had managed to free his gun. As the bear turned to claw the dog, Nansen fired and killed the animal. Fortunately Johansen and the dog suffered only minor scratches in the encounter. Before the excitement had passed, however, two large bear cubs appeared, seeking their mother. Johansen fired a shot at one, driving them off, but they returned and lingered in the area; they were still there when the men departed in their kayaks.

Two days after that incident, the party came to the edge of the drift ice. Across the water, in the distance, the land rose before them. The men were thrilled, but now they faced a

Johansen fought for his life

dreadful duty. The two surviving huskies could not be carried over the open sea in the kayaks. Neither, in good conscience, could the men leave the dogs, of whom they had become quite fond, to starve or to be hunted down by bears. So, compelled to act, yet reluctant to kill his own dog, each man shot the other's.

Then, with their kayaks tied together side by side to make a platform for the sleds, they paddled out to sea. They rigged a sail and made good progress. Crossing the water was easy compared with their recent struggles on the ice. As they drew nearer, the land they had seen turned out to be four islands largely covered with glaciers. Nansen named the first of them Eva's Island and the second, Liv's Island.

The travelers sailed on, sighting still more islands. They thought they had reached Franz Josef Land but weren't certain. Numbers of seabirds flew out to greet them: black-legged kittiwakes, ivory gulls, gray-white fulmars, and flocks of little black-and-white auks. They welcomed the sight of so much game.

The men continued in a southwesterly direction. At times ice floes blocked their passage, and they found it necessary to haul their kayaks and sleds over the ice again. At night they camped on drifting floes. They could navigate better now by separating the kayaks. So they shortened their sleds to fit separately across each of the boats and continued singly.

On the evening of August 15, they finally set foot on solid ground. The island where they landed had a rocky granite surface. It was such a joy to be on land once more that the men jumped around from stone to stone and frolicked like children. They found a bit of moss among the rocks and discovered some flowers in a protected niche. There were yellow poppies and saxifrages with large, purple blooms. They set up camp, planted the Norwegian flag, and feasted on lobscouse and the last of their potatoes.

On August 17 they came to another island. Here, at the

Land at last

edge of the cold, remote Arctic Ocean, Nansen walked along a flat beach strewn with seashells. In the clear, shallow water near shore, he observed snails and sea urchins and still farther out great masses of seaweed. Back on the shore, snow buntings leaped from rock to rock and little auks screeched from a bluff above. The men went exploring; they climbed a cliff and found scores of black-backed gulls nesting with their young.

They continued on their way until August 26, when an oncoming storm sent them scurrying ashore. Hurriedly the two set up camp, but the powerful winds destroyed their tent. The winds also brought ice to the coast, preventing them from leaving. The men had no choice but to make a shelter until they could depart. They pried stones loose from rubble beneath a glacier cliff and hauled them to a site where they built a crude stone hut. The tattered remains of their tent served for a roof, and they made a small entrance across which they hung their coats to block the wind. Inside there was barely enough room for the men to lie down, and Nansen's feet stuck out the door.

The next day, they were upset to find that ice blocked their exit southward in the direction they were heading. Because fall was rapidly approaching, this meant they could not expect to reach Spitsbergen in time to catch a boat home. What a blow this must have been to have their hopes of rejoining their loved ones soon dashed. But typical of Nansen, he made the practical decision to winter where they were and turned to the tough challenge of surviving in this bleak, inhospitable place without adequate shelter or provisions.

So the two explorers began to prepare for the cruel winter ahead. First, while there were still animals about, they hunted game to accumulate meat. They shot a number of polar bears and walruses. Slaughtering the huge, gray sea mammals was a repulsive job. They skinned the walruses for their hides and then removed the greasy blubber and the meat from the bulky carcasses; the blubber would be used for fuel. This messy work was done in shallow water where the bodies could easily be turned. When the men were finished, they were wet and covered with blood, oil, and fat.

By September 7 the team had stockpiled sufficient meat and blubber to begin their next task. They needed to build a more substantial hut. They would construct the hut in the Inuit manner, partly above and partly below ground. The men had few tools. They worked with the cut-off ends of the sled runners as picks, fashioned shovels from walrus shoulder blades, and used walrus tusks, ski poles, and crossbars from the sleds as other implements. They chose a site beneath a sheltering cliff and dug out a space three feet deep, six feet wide, and ten feet long.

On this foundation, they erected stone walls that rose three feet above the ground; this provided a room six feet high. They placed a pole of driftwood across the top and stretched walrus hides over this from side to side to make a roof. Stones held the hides in place. A narrow, underground passage that would later be roofed over by chunks of ice led into the hut. The outer end of this burrow was a hole in the ground covered with bearskin; the inner entrance had a bearskin door.

The weather grew steadily colder and snow began to fall. The men completed the hut and stored their supplies. They had killed eleven bears and several walruses by now and had ample meat and blubber.

On September 28 Nansen and Johansen moved from their temporary shelter into the relative luxury of their new winter home. Now they could walk around inside, and Nansen could almost stand up straight. Light and heat were provided by lamps that Nansen had formed from pieces of sheet metal that they carried to repair sled runners; camping matches, carefully conserved, were used to light them. The lamps had wicks made of cotton bandages and used bits of blubber for fuel. The hut was warm enough, they thought, to sleep in separate bags. So they divided their common sack, but their first night alone convinced them to sew the bags back together again. The bag was laid on a bench of stones, which was less than comfortable. The two also made a stone hearth on which to cook and formed a flue of rolled bearskin over it; the flue let the oily smoke out through a small hole cut in the roof. Over this, they would eventually add a chimney of packed snow and ice.

Nansen and Johansen took weekly turns cooking. Their menu never varied: boiled bear meat and soup for breakfast and fried bear steak for supper. Sometimes they ate bits of raw blubber or snacked on the burned ends of blubber from their oil lamps. "We called these cakes, and thought them uncommonly nice, and we were always talking of how delicious they would have been if we could have had a little sugar on them," Nansen wrote. The precious bags of flour, pemmican, bread, and chocolate that remained from their original provisions were buried outside for use in the spring when their journey south would resume. These caches were hidden under stones to protect them from animals, especially the clever arctic fox.

The arctic fox is a cunning little animal about the size of a large house cat. The foxes quickly discovered the explorers' base and raided it mercilessly. They made off with steel wire, harpoons, harpoon lines, and a ball of twine. The loss of the twine was particularly bothersome, for the men had hoped to use threads from it to sew winter clothes, socks, and a new sleeping bag. The little thieves even stole an outdoor thermometer. Camouflaged in their white winter coats, they looted at night. The men could hear them overhead on the roof of the hut gnawing at their stores of frozen meat. Once the birds had left and the bears departed in mid-October, the brazen bandits were the only visitors to come to the outpost all winter long.

On October 15 the sun disappeared below the horizon and the endless Arctic nights began once more. The explorers' lives settled into a routine. In the morning, after breakfast, they might venture outside in the dimness for a walk below the overhanging cliff to get some exercise. But fierce, frigid winds discouraged long excursions. Some days the gusts were so severe that the men barely poked their heads out of the burrow at all.

But they had to go out every few days, regardless of the weather, to get food, fuel, and ice. Melting ice supplied fresh water for drinking and preparing soup. Each venture outdoors in temperatures well below zero was numbing but made them appreciate their snug room all the more, even though the temperature inside barely rose above freezing.

The cold and monotony made the men sluggish. They had nothing to read but the almanac and some navigation tables that Nansen learned by heart. There was so little to write about that entries in their diaries became brief and irregular. The men slept a great deal, as much as twenty hours a day.

Despite their vastly different backgrounds, Nansen, the highly educated doctor of zoology and accomplished explorer, and Johansen, a reserve army lieutenant and former gymnast, got along remarkably well. Their common bond was the will to survive. Each valued the other, but for one minor problem. Johansen snored, and Nansen had to poke him constantly to get some sleep himself.

What did they talk about month after month in their small, one-room hut? They discussed the expedition and tried to figure out where the *Fram* was and when it might reach Norway. Nansen attempted to estimate how far the ship had drifted and where it might break out of the ice pack. He calculated that the *Fram* would arrive back home in midsummer or in the fall of 1896. He also worked on details for an expedition to Antarctica and the South Pole, where he planned to go after returning to Norway. The men spoke of home, memories, and their families. They talked about things they longed for—especially soap, a bath, and clean clothes.

Nansen and Johansen were completely covered from head to toe with dirt and grime. Their hair had grown long; they had thick, scruffy beards. Their greasy clothes stuck to them and caused sores. They would scrape dirt and fat from their skin with a knife. The grime that covered them could not be washed away with plain water. It took a scrubbing with warm bear's blood, a rinse in walrus oil, and a rub with dry moss to clean their caked hands.

Christmas and New Year's were celebrated with bits of chocolate; these were the only times they dipped into their spring caches. The new year, 1896, was ushered in by a wave of bitter cold; the temperature fell to minus 42.2 degrees

Fahrenheit. But gradually, as the weeks slipped by, the dim outside began to lighten. Birds started to return and, on February 29, the sun reappeared.

Soon polar bears began to wander by once more. Ice bears do not hibernate like other bears in winter; they venture instead out onto the drift ice to hunt while the pregnant females give birth to cubs in dens dug in the snow. One large, prowling male discovered the entrance to the explorers' hut. He poked his big paw through the outer cover and found the hidden passage. But Johansen took his rifle and shot the intruder before it could get any farther. Soon afterward, Nansen shot another bear. The two animals provided fresh meat to replenish the men's larder and helped to provision them for their journey ahead.

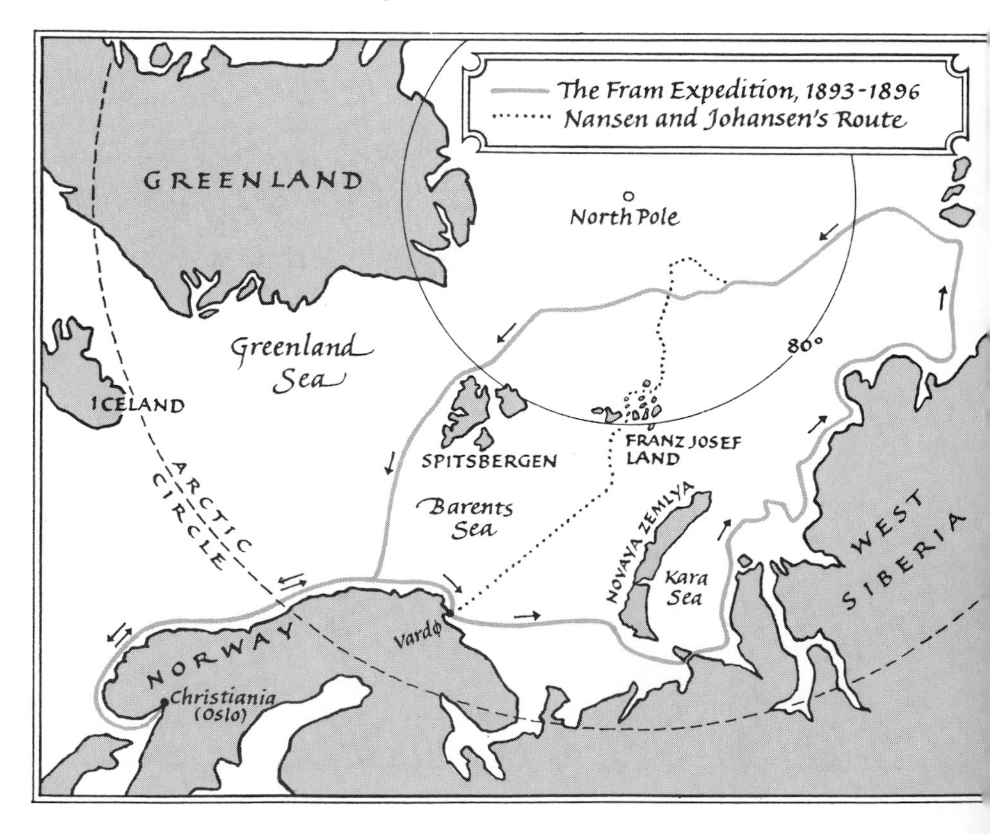

The return of daylight and the coming of spring revived the men. Eager for activity once more, the two busily made ready for the next leg of their trip. Both needed new clothes desperately, so ingeniously they unraveled their canvas bags for thread and sewed their old blankets into new garments. The men patched their worn wind clothes, made bearskin socks, gloves, and a new, lighter sleeping bag. They even managed to resole their summer boots with walrus hide. These tasks occupied them for weeks. Nansen and Johansen sat side by side in their sleeping bag in the dimly lit hut and sewed.

Nine long months had passed since the explorers had first come to the island, and they were anxious to move on. They retrieved their spring stores only to find that most of the provisions had become moldy and ruined. So they packed what was usable and their fresh supplies and lashed the kayaks atop the sleds. Finally, on May 19, the two were ready. Nansen wrote a brief history of the expedition, placed it in a brass tube from the cooker, and hung it from the ceiling of the hut. They bid their winter lair good-bye and hauled the sleds out onto the frozen channel.

They saw water sky in the southwest and hoped to reach it soon and sail all the way to Spitsbergen.

CHAPTER FIFTEEN

Homeward Journey

NANSEN AND JOHANSEN BEGAN the heavy work of towing their sleds over the ice again, this time unaided by dogs. But they were so out of condition from their many months of inactivity that they had to shorten their daily marches until their strength returned. Even so, the two were remarkably healthy. Neither had any signs of scurvy, the disease that had plagued so many Arctic explorers in the past. Their good health resulted from their diet of fresh meat, which contains vitamin C, the nutrient that prevents scurvy.

They rigged small sails on their sleds to take advantage of trailing winds as they moved down the flat, frozen channel between the islands to which they had come. On May 24, 1896, almost a week into this second leg of their homeward journey, signs of an approaching storm prompted them to land and find shelter. So while Johansen paused to take down his sail and secure it, Nansen raced ahead toward the nearest island to seek a campsite.

As he approached the shore, the ice became rough and broken. Cracks appeared; other splits, however, were hidden beneath a layer of snow. Suddenly, the surface under Nansen collapsed and his feet plunged through the ice into the frigid water below. He tried to pull them up again but couldn't; they were trapped under the ice by his skis. He leaned on his ski pole and used his free arm to support himself. But he was otherwise helpless, unable even to turn because his sled harness restrained him. He knew that it wouldn't take long for his feet to freeze and to be useless to him.

Never mind, Nansen told himself. Johansen had surely seen him fall and would come in a moment to pull him out. He tried to ignore the cold and the danger he was in. But then his ski pole sank farther, and he dropped still deeper into the icy water. With each passing second, his situation became more precarious. Where was Johansen? He couldn't wait any longer and began to call to his partner. No answer. He shouted again, louder, desperate now. But he only sank deeper. The water rose to his chest; his wet clothes grew heavy, pulling him down. He bellowed now with even greater urgency. Finally, his calls were answered. Johansen was there, creeping up cautiously behind him. Then the former athlete used his powerful arms and pulled him free.

For the next two weeks the explorers progressed over ice and water, alternately hauling the sleds or using the kayaks as conditions warranted. When the ice was smooth, they raised sail and skimmed along the surface. The men passed between a number of islands. Although still unsure that they were in Franz Josef Land, the two continued down the channel on a southwesterly course until they came out into open drift ice once more. It was June 11; the travelers were now south of the islands and water sky ahead encouraged them.

Early the following morning, they heard sounds that cheered them further. It was the noise of surf, of breakers. They had finally come to open sea. The men lashed their kayaks together and took to the water, sailing westward in the direction of Spitsbergen. They sailed all the rest of the day.

The trek southward

That evening they moored the boats to an ice floe and stopped to rest. Curious to see what conditions ahead might be, they climbed a hummock for a better view. But as they gazed out at the sea beyond, trouble struck. Johansen was the first to notice. The kayaks were gone; the boats, with all their food and equipment, had slipped free and drifted away, leaving the men marooned on the floe. If they could not retrieve them, the explorers knew they were doomed.

As fast as they could, the two scrambled down to the edge of the ice. Nansen handed Johansen his watch and quickly stripped off his outer clothes. Without delay, he plunged right into the frigid water. The clothes he still wore made swimming difficult, but he dared not remove them for fear the cold would cause him to cramp. Nansen swam after the kayaks. The wind, however, pushed them still farther away, maddeningly widening the gap he had to swim. It was agonizing to plow so clumsily through the icy water, but Nansen had no other choice. He might tire and drown, but he was certain to die anyway if he couldn't reach the boats.

The cold began to sap his energy. He turned over to swim on his back, hoping to conserve his stamina. He could see poor Johansen pacing up and down the floe behind, powerless to help. Nansen rolled over again. The kayaks were just ahead, closer, but his arms were now so stiff that he could hardly move them. He summoned up his dwindling strength and made a desperate lunge to seize hold of a ski lashed to the back of the boats. Grasping it with numb hands, he pulled himself alongside the kayaks. But did he have the energy left to haul his wooden body aboard? Nansen grabbed hold of a sled and, with all his might, managed to hoist himself up onto the deck of the boat.

He felt frozen and completely spent. He thought of untying the kayaks and towing one behind the other but decided against this. He was too chilled to take the time. So instead he attempted to maneuver the double craft single-handedly. This required scrambling back and forth to paddle first from one and then from the other boat. He succeeded in turning the kayaks and headed in toward the ice again. But then he did something almost insane.

Two auks were floating on the water nearby. Nansen spied the birds and determined that he would have them for his dwindling larder. So he found his rifle and shot them. The blasts startled Johansen, who was waiting anxiously on the floe. He wondered for an instant what had possessed his companion until he saw Nansen retrieve the birds.

By the time he reached the ice, Nansen was so weak he could barely crawl ashore. But Johansen peeled off his wet clothes, dressed him in dry things, and helped him into the sleeping bag to rest and get warm. While his exhausted partner slept, Johansen set up camp, cooked the birds, and made soup. The hot meal the two shared that night did much to

Hoisting himself aboard the boat

ease their recent ordeal. But Johansen would remember the incident as "the worst moments" of his life.

The following evening, when the tide was right, the explorers sailed on again, heading west. They made good progress, although they stopped to shoot and slaughter two walruses along the way. The men separated the kayaks, finding it easier to travel faster singly. They maintained a good pace until morning when they began to encounter individual walruses in the water. Although walruses are generally content to feed on crabs, clams, and other bottom creatures, there are some that prey on seals; these are usually lone males that sometimes upset small boats and attack people thrown into the water. So all that day and on through the night, the men were forced to proceed warily along the edge of the ice where they could quickly escape for protection.

Then near morning, on June 16, Johansen, who was leading, spotted a single walrus in the water ahead of them. Sensing danger, he put in to the ice. Although less concerned, Nansen turned to follow his partner. The walrus ducked under and vanished. Then all of a sudden, it popped up next to Nansen. It raised a great flipper onto the front edge of the kayak and tried to tip the boat over. Nansen struggled to hold on and keep the kayak righted. He took his paddle and struck the walrus on the head, battling to drive it off. But the stubborn animal only reached farther across the boat and, using its weight, pressed the front of the kayak down still deeper. Nansen could see the walrus's sharp tusks ready to tear into the canvas shell of the boat. He put down his paddle and reached for his gun. He was going to shoot, but before he could, the walrus let go and ducked into the water again.

Nansen breathed easier for a moment. Then he felt a cold wetness on his legs and heard the ominous sound of water trickling into the boat. The walrus had gashed the fragile craft, after all. The boat was taking on water and sinking quickly. Without delay, Nansen paddled the few strokes to the ice and, with Johansen's help, managed to lift the damaged craft up out of the water.

The explorers patched the kayak and camped on the ice. Early the next afternoon, June 17, Nansen climbed a hummock to view an island nearby. A covering mist had lifted and he studied the rocky isle, observing its glaciers and ice fields. Thousands of birds circled overhead. The air was filled with their screeching. Then he thought he heard another sound muffled by the raucous noise. Nansen listened carefully; he couldn't be sure. Perhaps it was only his imagination fooling him, but he thought he had heard a dog. He strained to hear it again. The only sound, however, was the birds. He waited, listening. There it was again. This time he was certain. What he heard was clearly the sound of dogs barking. He hurried to tell Johansen.

Johansen realized instantly that dogs would not be here in this remote place alone; people would be with them. But nothing seemed more unlikely. He listened carefully himself, but he heard only the squeals of the auks and kittiwakes flying above. Surely Nansen must be mistaken.

The two talked the matter over. They ate and, although Johansen remained unconvinced, he agreed to stay with the kayaks while Nansen took his telescope and gun and went off to investigate. Nansen trekked through the snow in the direction from which the barking had come. He had gone only a short distance, however, when he came upon fresh animal tracks. They seemed too large to have been made by an arctic fox; they were more the size of a wolf's or a dog's. This puzzled Nansen. Surely if a dog had come this close to their campsite, it would have barked and made itself known. But his thoughts were abruptly interrupted by the unmistakable yelping of a dog. Thrilled, he hastened toward the noise. Now he heard what sounded like a human voice, too. With his heart pounding, Nansen scampered up a hummock and called out as loud as he could. There, in the distance, was a dog and, farther behind it, the figure of a man.

Seeing each other, the two men waved their hats and hurried toward each other. The stranger was neatly dressed in high rubber boots and a checked, woolen suit. He was well groomed, clean shaven, and even smelled of scented soap. Nansen heard him speak to the dog in English. He recognized the man almost immediately as Frederick Jackson, an explorer he had met in London.

With almost comic formality, considering it all, the elegant Briton and the savage-looking Norwegian in his grimy, tattered rags faced each other and politely exchanged greetings: "How do you do?"

"I'm immensely glad to see you," said Jackson, with typically good English manners.

"Thank you; I also," replied Nansen, mistakenly assuming that the other had remembered him.

They chatted for a few minutes; then the Englishman suddenly asked: "Aren't you Nansen?"

"Yes, I am."

"By Jove! I am glad to see you!" said Jackson finally, showing his excitement. He walked Nansen back to his camp and assured him that Eva and Liv had been well when he had left London for the Arctic two years earlier. At camp he

Meeting Jackson, reenacted six days later

introduced Nansen to other members of his party. He also sent men off to pick up Johansen.

Nansen learned that he was indeed in Franz Josef Land, in the southwestern corner of the chain of islands; the English team had been exploring this area for the past nineteen months. It turned out, in fact, that Jackson had trekked to within thirty-five miles of the Norwegians' winter hut without any knowledge that Nansen and Johansen had been nearby.

The English camp was a comfortable log cabin. It had a green cloth roof and walls that were further decorated with pictures and shelves filled with books. A coal-fired stove provided ample warmth; it was an altogether civilized place, and a far cry from the Norwegians' primitive winter lair. Nansen sat in a comfortable chair. Jackson handed him a tin box of letters that he had been carrying just in case their paths crossed. In it was a newsy letter from Nansen's brother, Alexander, that cheered him enormously.

The Norwegians were well treated by their British hosts. They dined with them and enjoyed many foods they had missed, including bread, butter, coffee, milk, and sugar. They bathed, shaved, cut their hair, and enjoyed clean, soft clothes again. Both men found that they had gained weight in the fifteen months since they had left the *Fram* despite the rigors of having traveled some seven hundred miles; Nansen had put on twenty-two pounds and Johansen, thirteen.

They checked the time and found that the estimates they had made when their watches unwound were fairly accurate. The confusion that they had about their location had stemmed more from errors on Payer's maps. Payer, it seemed, had mistaken dense clouds of mist in certain places for glacier-covered islands.

Nansen and Johansen remained in the British camp until midsummer. On July 26 a steamer, the *Windward,* arrived to resupply the Jackson expedition. Eager for news, all the men

Johansen arrives at Jackson's base

plied the ship's captain with questions. They learned what had happened back in the world they had left behind. A war had been fought in the Far East between China and Japan. New technologies had been developed: the X-ray machine, wireless telegraphy, and color photography.

The *Windward* departed on August 7 with the two Norwegians aboard. Three years had passed since Nansen had said good-bye to his wife and infant daughter, and he longed to be with them again. Both men ached to see their homeland once more. Finally on August 12, Nansen "saw something dark ahead, low down on the horizon . . . It was land, it was Norway!"

The small island harbor of Vardø on Norway's far northern coast was the *Windward*'s first port of call. She anchored there on August 13. Vardø is a modest town with a few shops, a hotel, and a telegraph office to which Nansen and Johansen hastened on landing. They dispatched telegrams, first to Eva and to Johansen's mother. Then they sent word of their return to the king, government officials, and others concerned with the expedition.

The manager of the telegraph station was thrilled to greet the explorers. He told them that there was a guest at the hotel in Vardø just then who undoubtedly would also be eager to see them, a Professor Mohn. By coincidence or fate, the very man whose theory had inspired Nansen was there in Vardø at his return. Nansen was elated. The reunion with Mohn was joyful and celebrated with champagne.

From Vardø, Nansen and Johansen took a coastal steamer to the sealing port of Hammerfest. Here in Norway's northernmost city, Nansen met his beloved Eva. She had come north by another coastal steamer to join him immediately on receiving his telegram. A British friend, Sir George Baden-Powell, happened to be in the harbor at that time aboard his yacht, the *Otaria*. Baden-Powell was so delighted to see Nansen that he generously invited the explorers and Eva to share the luxurious yacht with him. Wires of greetings and congratulations came flooding in. But there was no word of the *Fram*. Nansen began to worry that she might not arrive before the fall had passed. On August 20, however, he received this telegram:

Fridtjof Nansen:

Fram arrived in good condition. All well on board. Shall start at once for Tromsö. Welcome home!

Otto Sverdrup.

Nansen and Johansen were beside themselves with joy. Along with their host, his wife, and Eva, they promptly set sail for Tromsø. When they reached port, the *Fram* was already there. After seventeen months' separation, the thirteen members of the expedition were finally all back in Norway together again. The *Fram* had traveled with the ice pack, just as Nansen had foreseen. His plan for the expedition was proven. Although the *Fram* had not crossed the Pole, it had reached as far as 85°55.5′ north latitude on November 15, 1895. It broke out of the ice near Spitsbergen, as Nansen had predicted; it did so on August 13, the very day he and Johansen had landed in Vardø. So thirteen indeed was the expedition's lucky number.

Johansen rejoined the crew on the *Fram* while Nansen remained with Eva aboard the yacht. Led by a government tugboat, the *Fram,* with the yacht trailing behind, departed for the journey down the long Norwegian coast. It was a procession hailed by every town and hamlet along the way. At stops in the port cities of Trondheim and Bergen, festive receptions welcomed them.

The *Fram* reached Christiania Fjord on September 9; Nansen reboarded her here for the final leg of the journey. The ship, however, made a small detour to stop and honor its builder, Colin Archer; then it continued up the fjord toward the capital. Patrol boats, warships, and steamers crowded with cheering people came out to escort her into harbor.

The wharves of the old port, the walls of the ancient Akershus Castle, and Christiania's streets teemed, as never before, with greeters eager to see the *Fram* and its heroes.

Their return was celebrated with thirteen gun blasts from three men-of-war and a battery of cannons on the Akershus; thirteen salvos were fired, one to salute each of the thirteen explorers. Ashore, a spirited reception awaited them. There were gaiety and welcomes by delegations of officials. Bands played, the national anthem was sung, and there was plenty of speech making. But Nansen's eyes were on a little three-and-a-half-year-old girl eager to meet her father. Then there followed a parade, a greeting at the royal palace by the king, and many receptions, parties, and festivities.

At home, at last, Nansen felt finally at peace. He was happy to be with his family once more. He savored memories of his great adventure: "The ice and the long moonlit polar nights, with all their yearning, seemed like a far-off dream from another world—a dream that had come and passed away. But what would life be worth without its dreams?" he mused.

On February 7, 1897, Nansen was feted once again at the Savage Club in London. He entertained his "Brother Savages" with humorous and harrowing stories of his polar adventures. But then he remembered that he had a promise to fulfill. So he took a pencil, turned, and proudly wrote his name and the date again on the wall above the inscription he had written four years earlier. He added to it a small map of the polar region and, on it, marked the place, 86°14′ N, that he and Johansen had reached and the date, April 8, 1895, they had arrived there.

Afterword

NANSEN WAS HONORED with many medals and awards from all over the world for the success of his expedition; the Prince of Wales, soon to be King of England, presented him with a special gold medal on behalf of the Royal Geographical Society. For a time he gave further thought to making a trek to the South Pole, but that wasn't to be. Instead he committed himself to lecturing, writing, scientific activities, and family matters.

The Nansens had four more children after Liv and soon required a larger home. Nansen designed a grand house for them, a brick mansion with a tower from which he could look out onto the fjord. It was built amid acres of parkland, yet it was less than five miles from the center of Christiania. He named it *Polhogda,* or Polar Heights, and moved the family there when it was finished in 1900.

Nansen became Professor of Zoology at Christiania University and lectured there and abroad, in Europe and America. He wrote a two-volume history of his polar journey titled *Farthest North* and also published six scholarly books on the scientific research of his expedition. In 1900, he went on an oceanographic research cruise in the Arctic Ocean.

The turn of the century brought new developments in politics that were to lure Nansen away from his usual pursuits. He became a leader in efforts to separate his homeland from its union with Sweden and, in 1905, helped Norway to gain its independence peacefully. Nansen accepted the honor of becoming Norway's first ambassador to Great Britain. He served there, in London, from 1906 to 1908 when, after a brief illness, Eva, who was only forty-nine, died, and he came home to his children.

Nansen returned to teaching and to his scientific career. He became Professor of Oceanography at the university, invented oceanographic instruments, and made a number of research cruises until the outbreak of World War I (1914–1918) halted these voyages. In 1919 Nansen remarried and took leave of his academic work to serve his country as a diplomat once more.

He became Norway's delegate to the League of Nations, the international organization formed in the aftermath of the war to promote peace. The League was the forerunner of the present United Nations organization and it was based in Geneva, Switzerland. Nansen committed his energies to the enormous problem of helping prisoners of war to return to their homelands and to the even greater task of finding places for the millions of people who had become homeless as a result of the war and of the Russian Revolution (1917). He worked tirelessly in 1920 and 1921 to resettle these refugees, creating papers for them. "Nansen Passports," as they became known, permitted them to enter and to settle in other countries. In 1922 he took on the plight of thousands of starving Russian, Greek, and Armenian displaced persons and tried to bring them food and relief.

In recognition of these selfless humanitarian efforts, Nansen was awarded the Nobel Peace Prize in Christiania on December 10, 1922. In his dedication to the unfortunate victims of wars and catastrophes, Nansen may have found the

Ambassador to Great Britain

purpose of his life that he had so long sought. He worked for the League of Nations for a few more years, but he also took time to continue writing scientific papers and books, many of which he illustrated himself. His sacrifices on behalf of the needy, however, had taken a toll on his health; his heart weakened. He died at home, at Polhogda, on May 13, 1930, at the age of sixty-eight.

The final resting place of this daring athlete, explorer, author, artist, scientist, diplomat, and humanitarian was in the garden of his home as he had wished. So ended the saga of this modern Viking. The boy who had been given the strange and ancient name, Fridtjof, that no other child was likely to know, had become famous the world over.

Notes

Page 1. *Oslo*. In 1925, Christiania reverted to its original ancient Viking name.

Page 4. *Skiing*. Skiing was invented some 4,000 years ago by ancient Norsemen. In modern times, up to about 1890, Norwegians continued to use a single pole. But as skiing became a popular sport, skiers began to use two poles. Two-pole skiing was common by the time the sport spread widely to other European and North American countries.

Page 17. *Greenland*. Greenland is about equal in size to the area of the United States east of the Mississippi River, approximately 840,000 square miles. Some 700,000 square miles of this territory is covered with ice. Greenland's ice cap is second in size only to Antarctica's and is as much as 10,000 feet deep in places.

Page 25. *Eskimo*. The term *Eskimo* comes from the French word *Esquimau*. It means "an eater of raw flesh" and was commonly used by Canadian Indians to describe their native Arctic neighbors. Today these people prefer their own tribal names. Those in the northeastern provinces of Canada and in Greenland are called *Inuit* which, in their tongue, means "the people."

Page 53. *Ice cap*. The difference between day and night temperatures at higher elevations on the Greenland ice cap can be as much as 40 degrees Fahrenheit. This remarkable spread exists in few other places in the world. One of these is the Sahara desert in North Africa.

Page 59. *Coracle.* The coracle, a sled, skis, poles, and other bits of equipment from the Greenland expedition can be seen at the Ski Museum in Holmenkollen, a suburb of Oslo.

Page 63. *Inuit friends.* Nansen said good-bye to his Inuit friends in Greenland but never forgot them. Each Christmas, he sent them greetings and gifts.

Page 65. *May 30.* In the cheering throngs that greeted Nansen on May 30, 1889, upon his return from Greenland, was seventeen-year-old Roald Amundsen. Inspired by Nansen, Amundsen would achieve fame as an explorer himself. In 1903–1906 he would be the first to navigate the Northwest Passage and, in 1911, the first to reach the South Pole.

Page 72. *Spitsbergen.* Spitsbergen is the name of both a group of islands and the largest island among them; the archipelago is also known by the Norwegian name Svalbard (meaning "cold coast").

Franklin. The vanished Franklin expedition was sought for years. Teams from England and America scoured the Canadian Arctic for the lost men until finally, in 1859, a British sled party under the command of the explorer Francis M'Clintock recovered the only written record of their fate. Franklin's two ships had been trapped in the ice and abandoned. The note revealed the deaths of Franklin and twenty-three of his officers and men. The author and the remaining members of the crew perished later from exposure, starvation, and other miseries.

Page 73. *Scurvy.* Vitamin C, which prevents scurvy, is not produced in the human body and must be taken in regularly to keep the tissues from breaking down. By the end of the eighteenth century, sailors and others had learned that fresh fruits prevented the disease. But Arctic explorers couldn't take perishables on their long journeys, and the canned lemon and lime juices they relied upon were often inadequate. Pemmican, the staple of sled journeys, was also lacking in vitamin C and those who depended solely upon it got scurvy. Little notice was taken of the fact that the Inuit who ate no fresh fruits or vegetables were somehow protected from the disease. Nansen and Johansen avoided scurvy because they hunted and ate fresh meat, rich in vitamin C, as the Inuit did.

Page 76. *The New Siberian Islands.* The New Siberian Islands, an icy wasteland today, once enjoyed a mild climate and were covered with grassy plains. The extinct northern species of elephant, the woolly mammoth, the hairy rhinoceros, and the buffalo grazed the islands until some twelve thousand years ago when they were trapped and destroyed by glaciers. Since the early 1800s, Russian ivory collectors have visited the islands to gather the tusks and bones of the ancient mammoths.

Page 78. *Sovereign.* Over the course of its history, Norway was dominated by its neighbors, Denmark and Sweden. In the period 1814 to 1905, Norway and Sweden were united under the King, or Sovereign, of Sweden.

Page 81. *The* Fram. The *Fram* was used by others after Nansen's epic voyage. From 1898 to 1902, Otto Sverdrup took her to map the northwest coast of Greenland. Under the command of Roald Amundsen, the *Fram* achieved a new record for exploration in 1911: she sailed farther south than any other ship of her time. On this expedition to Antarctica, Amundsen and his team from the *Fram* went on by dogsled to reach the South Pole. Today the *Fram* can be visited ashore at the Fram Museum that was constructed over her at Bygdøy, Oslo. In this museum one of the sleds and one of the kayaks used by Johansen and Nansen can also be seen, together with different instruments and articles used by Nansen.

Page 82. *Admiral Sir George Nares.* As a naval captain, Nares had led a British expedition (1875–1876) in the North American Arctic that reached 83°20′ north latitude, a record to that time.

Page 83. *General Adolphus Greely.* When Greely was an army lieutenant, he had led an American expedition in the same area as Nares and in 1883 reached 83°24′ north latitude, beating the British best by four miles. Nansen and Johansen would exceed his polar quest by some one hundred and seventy miles.

Page 84. *Champion gymnast.* Johansen had competed in athletic competitions as a gymnast. At a meet in Paris, he was awarded a gold medal for an amazing somersault over forty-two men.

Page 154. *Oceanographic instruments.* Nansen, one of the pioneers of modern oceanography, invented several devices useful for research. The best known is the "Nansen Bottle," an instrument consisting of several tubes that is lowered into the sea to collect water samples and to determine temperatures at different depths.

Bibliography

American Museum of Natural History. Eskimo Exhibit. New York.

Bain, J. Arthur. *Life and Exploration of Fridtjof Nansen.* London: Walter Scott, Ltd., 1897.

Berton, Pierre. *The Arctic Grail.* New York: Viking, 1988.

Brögger, W. C., and Nordahl Rolfsen. *Fridtjof Nansen, 1861–1893.* London, New York, and Bombay: Longmans, Green and Co., 1896.

Fram Museum. Bygdøy, Oslo, Norway.

Hall, Sam. *The Fourth World.* New York: Alfred A. Knopf, 1987.

Høyer, Liv Nansen. *Nansen, A Family Portrait.* London: Longmans, Green and Co., 1957.

Huntford, Roland. *The Last Place on Earth.* New York: Atheneum, 1985.

Jackson, Frederick G. *A Thousand Days in the Arctic.* New York and London: Harper & Brothers, 1899.

Jones, Gwyn. *The Norse Atlantic Saga.* London: Oxford University Press, 1964.

Lopez, Barry. *Arctic Dreams.* Toronto, New York, London, Sydney, Auckland: Bantam Books, 1987.

Maxtone-Graham, John. *Safe Return Doubtful.* New York: Charles Scribner's Sons, 1988.

Nansen, Fridtjof. *The First Crossing of Greenland.* 2 vols. London and New York: Longmans, Green and Co., 1890.

———. *Eskimo Life.* London: Longmans, Green and Co., 1893.

———. *Farthest North.* 2 vols. New York and London: Harper & Brothers, 1897.

———. *Hunting and Adventure in the Arctic*. New York: Duffield and Company, 1925.

New York Times. November 13, 1896; December 6, 1896; February 7, 1897; February 9, 1897; May 14, 1930; May 15, 1930; May 18, 1930.

Ski Museum. Holmenkollen, Norway.

Sörensen, Jon. *The Saga of Fridtjof Nansen*. New York: The American-Scandinavian Foundation, W. W. Norton & Company, 1932.

Stefansson, Vilhjalmur. *Great Adventures and Explorations*. New York: Dial Press, 1952.

Whitehouse, J. Howard, ed. *Nansen, A Book of Homage*. London: Hodder and Stoughton, 1930.

Index